AND THEY TOOK THEMSELVES WIVES

And They Took Themselves Wives

The Emergence of Patriarchy in
Western Civilization

DAVID BAKAN

1817

Published in San Francisco by Harper & Row, Publishers

New York / Hagerstown / San Francisco / London

*To the memory of
my parents*

FIRST EDITION

Designer: Jim Mennick

Library of Congress Cataloging in Publication Data

Bakan, David.
    AND THEY TOOK THEMSELVES WIVES.

    Includes bibliographical references and index.
    1. Patriarchy. 2. Family—Biblical teaching.
I. Title.
HQ756.B34 1979   301.42   79-1763
ISBN 0-06-060360-7

---

79 80 81 82 83 10 9 8 7 6 5 4 3 2 1

Contents

CHAPTER 1

Introduction

In this book I will consider the notions of marriage and the family in the Bible, and, through an interpretive exercise, attempt to better appreciate their bearing on some of the social problems of the contemporary world. The author of the historical background section of the article on "Family and Marriage" of *The New Encyclopaedia Britannica* (1977 edition) asserts that "The family pattern of the patriarchs, as described in the Bible, still influences present practices. Abraham, Isaac and Jacob are described as nomad chieftains, owning great herds, married to several wives, allowed to take concubines and to get rid of them. The Old Testament accorded women a lower status than men and, in some respects, so did Christianity." This passage shows clearly that we must interpret the Bible at a high level of abstraction to understand its relationship to the contemporary world. For while it is undoubtedly true that the "family pattern of the patriarchs ... still influences present practices," men are no longer nomad chieftains, owners of great herds, or polygamous, and the institution of concubinage does not exist in modern countries. Thus, such influence must be of a kind that transcends these concrete practices and relationships.

Even with this abiding influence, the institution of marriage, at the present time, appears to be undergoing substantial change. A deeper understanding of these current changes might be possible if we are able to grasp the meaning of the biblical text at more depth.

For, if there is a "written constitution" for the institution of marriage anywhere in Western civilization, it is the Bible.

Many observers have suggested that we are currently in a general period of change and transition as great, perhaps, as the world has experienced since the Renaissance and the Reformation. Changes abound in the political and economic spheres. These changes entail corresponding changes in the social sphere, within which lies the institution of marriage.

What is the common ideal of the family that we associate with the Bible? Sexually, the norm is virginity prior to marriage, with all sexual relations limited to married heterosexual couples. Great significance is assigned to the female's virginity prior to marriage and to her fidelity after marriage. Fundamental authority within the family resides in the husband-father. Children are expected to be deferent to their parents, and the wife-mother is expected to be deferent to the husband-father. Social status and material inheritance from parents to children are usually transmitted patrilineally. Parents are obliged to provide maintenance, protection, and education for the children. The husband-father is primarily responsible for bringing outside resources into the household not least, to toil and sweat for food (Genesis 3:17–19). The wife-mother is responsible for production of in-house resources, and the appropriate use of resources in housekeeping and nursing. Physical nurturance and protection against everyday dangers rests primarily with the wife-mother. Protection against outside dangers, such as marauders and predators, is largely the responsibility of the husband-father. Early education of the children rests with the wife-mother; while later education, particularly of the male children, is the obligation of the husband-father.

Is this patriarchal idea unqualified in the Biblical text? I suggest that it is not. The Bible contains numerous counterindications. One of the major contributions to the understanding of the Bible has been the development of the so-called documentary hypothesis, an assertion that the Bible was drawn together from many relatively independent documents, and edited. Scholars accepting the documentary hypothesis have attempted detailed identification of different parts. If we accept the hypothesis, and the sequence of the documents that has been suggested, it then appears that the strong patriarchal idea of marriage is associated largely with P, the priestly author of relatively late date. The earlier documents appear to express norms which are more matrilineal, matrilocal, and even matriarchal. I will return to this point in detail presently.

The authority of the Bible is hardly as powerful today as it has been at other times in the history of Western civilization. But whether the norms of the Bible are followed or rejected, they still constitute a profoundly important presence in the culture of the contemporary world. I do not believe that the norms were ever arbitrary. They emerged out of historical life conditions. They performed important functions, although some important trade-offs were connected with them. They moved through understandable developmental patterns. They informed the developmental patterns of cultural history, as well as individual life patterns within that cultural history.

In this book I will attempt to explicate some themes that appear to me to be just beneath the surface of the Bible. What is beneath the surface may not have the authority of explicit commandment, yet it is real as an influence. As I have worked in preparing this book, the thought often occurred to me that these beneath-the-surface themes may be precisely the ones that are gaining dominance at the present time. The rejection of the authority of the Bible which is so often evident appeared to me as the rejection of manifest norms; while the power of the beneath-the-surface injunctions continues to play a role. Paradoxically, even the rejection of the explicit biblical authority sometimes seems consonant with these beneath-the-surface themes.

Many of the thoughts I will express have been developing in my mind for a long time. I would like to share with the reader some of the events that brought me to the point of deliberately expressing them.

I had been asked by a local association of homosexuals to give a talk on sex and sex differences, a topic to which I had once devoted some attention.[1] Some days after I gave the talk I received a phone call from a woman who had been in the audience. She asked if I would see her about a certain matter, and I agreed. She brought a friend with her. Both women were in their middle thirties and had been living together in a homosexual relationship for ten years. They told me they wanted to have a child—not an adopted child, but one of their own. They had not settled the question of which of them was to become pregnant or who the "donor" was to be. But these they considered minor questions. The major question on their minds was what would be the psychological consequences for a child born and raised in such a household? My reply was hedged. I mumbled some things about the future of public acceptance of their kind of relationship and about the kind of care and affection they could provide the child. And when I asked them *why* they wanted to have a child, they replied, "Why does any couple want to have a child?"

Another incident involved a young man, a student, who had been living with a young woman for three years. When he opened the conversation on this topic, I could not refrain from asking him why they did not get married. His reply to me was, "Dr. Bakan, what is marriage?" Recognizing that his question was rhetorical, I asked him to tell me. "Marriage," he said, "is cohabitation with the permission of the church or the state. I have no respect for either. I do not need their permission." At that moment the thought of Abraham came into my mind. Abraham's marriage, I recalled, was *in defiance* of the state. The text recounts how Abraham twice found it wise—as did Isaac on one occasion—to conceal his marriage from the state to save his life (Genesis 12:10 ff.; 20:1 ff.; 26:6 ff.). The student continued, "If we have children, they will be legitimate because they exist, and not because the church or state says so."

A female student in one of my classes once openly boasted to the class about how effectively she was raising her child born out of wedlock. Another female student deliberately planned to have, and had, a child out of wedlock. She said that she wanted a child but did not want a husband. Having a child, she said, was her destiny; but having a husband was not.

In each of these cases I noted a capacity for loving children and a realism beyond the guilt associated with violating the long-standing social norms of our society. The deviant norms did not seem to be drawn from tradition or from abstract principle. Rather, their decisions arose from assessment of situation and consequence, and each individual's particular existential longings.

On the surface all these people certainly seemed to reject the norms of the classical Judeo-Christian tradition. And yet, I could not but feel that, in some sense, they were within it. They possessed that convergence of caring, sense of destiny, and responsiveness to conscience that, in my opinion, is characteristic of the Judeo-Christian tradition. I would have found it very hard to argue that there was less commitment to children in these cases than in any number of traditional marriages I have known.

I found myself asking several questions: What features of the contemporary world could allow such historically deviant patterns to take place? Is the written "constitution" of marriage in Western civilization really being violated? And if we project such trends into the future, what consequences are there for human ethical and existential fulfillment, and for the fate of society at large?

This book is my attempt to grapple with these questions. The answer to the first question may be easily reached—it is common "social science" knowledge. This question will be discussed in Chapter 2. The second question is more difficult. For me, the key is in recognizing that the Judeo-Christian tradition is complex, and that the biblical text is a developmental record as well as an expression of a single ideological and spiritual point of view. Chapter 3 indicates the importance of the theme of paternity, the male's biological involvement in the birth of a child, as a basis for various other considerations in the minds of the biblical authors. Chapter 4 gives an overview of the developmental sequence that the biblical text suggests to me and summarizes my main argument concerning the Bible. Chapter 5 provides some background for examining the biblical text. Chapter 5 may be skipped or skimmed by those who are already acquainted with this background. Chapter 6 explicates my approach to the interpretive task generally. In Chapters 7, 8, and 9

I deal directly with the biblical text. Chapter 10 constitutes my attempt to speak to the third question, the possibilities for the future.

NOTES

1. David Bakan, *The Duality of Human Existence* (Boston: Beacon Press, 1966), especially Chapter 4, "Agency and Communion in Human Sexuality."

CHAPTER 2

The Contemporary Situation and Family Roles

Are we, in this second half of the twentieth century, at a major historical turning point? I think that we are.

We have come to the virtual end of global expansion into previously sparsely occupied land. At the end of the eighteenth century Thomas Malthus clearly set forth the problem of the relationship between limited resources and population size. He indicated the variety of disasters that could arise as population growth pushed against the limits of available resources. While huge new untouched sources of land were available when Malthus wrote, there are few such tracts now. The planet is quite occupied. There are more living people on the earth at the present time than at any earlier time. The great technology we have developed to extract sustenance from the earth has produced great dangers of exhaustion of raw materials and convulsive upsets to ecological balance. We have to perform some great new technological miracles or quickly modify our political, economic, and social arrangements. Technological miracles may perhaps be forthcoming, but planning on the basis of anticipated miracles of any kind is hardly a wise strategy. Indeed, we must also consider the possibility that science's ability to contribute positively to social welfare is no longer what it used to be—or at least what we once thought it to be.

We must recognize that it is precisely the family, and the traditional norms for the family, that critically enter into the planet's formula for population change and resource use.

The contemporary world is characterized by an international political situation different from what it has been in the past. The hegemony of Europe gave way to that of America and the Soviet Union, which in turn has to come to terms with powers in Asia and Africa. Since the Bible is the basis for many norms in European culture, the decline of European hegemony may well entail a decline in the significance of this Judeo-Christian tradition in the world.

There is fabulously increased world contact among all people and enormous interdependence among all people on the planet. Whereas at earlier times in history, significant political economic and social involvements of people took place within relatively small groups, today the group of significant people for each individual is the whole population of the planet. Communication, trade, and transportation networks put every person in contact with virtually every other person in the world. We use goods from virtually every point on the planet, and almost any manufactured product is the result of the coordinated labor of millions of people all over the world.

Historically, the most significant basic unit within the state was the traditional family. State governments interacted primarily with heads of families rather than with individuals. However, the significance of the familial subunit has declined and the state increasingly interacts with the individual in the modern world.

The number of years of life that an individual spends on the planet as an adult has substantially increased over the last century, and may increase even further in the near future. Maturation is more rapid, and death comes later. For example, the average age for the onset of menstruation was over seventeen a hundred years ago. Now it is under thirteen.[1] The reduction of the voting age is an implicit recognition of the trend to earlier maturity. At the same time, length of life has increased greatly. The table below shows life expectancy for white males and females, for various adult ages, for 1900–1902 and 1976. The changes for both sexes are positive at all ages. However, the gains for women exceed the gains for men. Thus "until death do us part" has been extended for both sexes, but the chances of a female outliving her spouse have risen too.

Average number of years of life remaining for white males and females*

Age	Sex	1900–1902	1976	Change (years)
15	M	46.25	56.2	+ 9.95
	F	47.79	63.6	+15.81
20	M	42.19	51.6	+ 9.41
	F	43.77	58.7	+14.93
25	M	38.52	47.1	+ 8.58
	F	40.05	53.9	+13.85
30	M	34.88	42.4	+ 7.52
	F	36.42	49.1	+12.68
35	M	31.29	37.7	+ 6.41
	F	32.82	44.2	+11.38
45	M	24.21	28.7	+ 4.49
	F	25.41	34.9	+ 9.49
60	M	14.35	16.9	+ 2.55
	F	15.23	22.0	+ 6.77

*Data drawn from *Vital Statistics of the United States,* 1976. Volume II, Section 5, *Life Tables.* Hyattsville, Maryland: U.S. Department of Health, Education and Welfare, 1978, Table 5–4, page 5–14.

Participation of women in the labor force has also increased. Women constituted 40 percent of the labor force in 1974, whereas a decade before it was about 30 percent. It will certainly continue to increase.

There has been a steady shift, corresponding to the great growth of urbanization in the last century, of satisfaction of basic needs from the family to the market and the larger society. Publicly available now are nursing, medical, social and psychological services; prepared goods such as food; clothing; shelter; recreation; education; and protection. Indeed, the family is often relegated to a consumption cooperative and congeniality association. The critical role of the family-household in providing essential maintenance, protection, and education functions, on which life itself often depended in the past, no longer prevails.

Children are of substantially reduced value to parents than they were in America two centuries ago. Adam Smith, who wrote his *Wealth of Nations* around the time of the American Revolution, spoke of the economic value of children in America at that time:

> Those who live to old age, it is said, frequently see there some fifty to a hundred, and sometimes many more, descendants from their own body. Labor is there so well rewarded that a numerous family of children, instead of being a burden is a source of opulence and prosperity to the parents. The labor of each child, before it can leave their house, is computed to be worth a hundred pounds clear gain to them. A young widow with four or five young children, who, among the middling or inferior ranks of people in Europe, would have so little chance for a second husband, is there frequently courted as a sort of fortune. The value of children is the greatest of all encouragements to marriage. We cannot, therefore, wonder that the people of North America should generally marry very young.[2]

In modern industrial society, the economic value of children to their parents is generally either null or negative. Children are not economic producers. They do not provide security in old age; varieties of arrangements have replaced support for the aged by children. Children consume a great proportion of the income brought in by the working members of a household. A child in America, for example, can be counted as an economic liability of at least $50,000 in direct costs, and considerably more if the income-producing capacity of a mother who stays out of the labor force to engage in child care is taken into account. The existential rewards of parenthood, the gratification associated with giving life and all that goes with it, come at increasingly greater economic costs.

The value of parents to children, with the possible exception of very early childhood, is also in decline. The larger society has come to assume more and more of the responsibility for the fundamental maintenance, protection, and education of children. Every form of social status must increasingly be gained independently by young people. Income, gift, and inheritance taxes have considerably reduced the capacity of parents to pass wealth on to their children. Even parental inculcation of values and attitudes is often perceived as detrimental rather than advantageous by young people confronting a rapidly changing society.

Last, but hardly least, in this enumeration, the increased availability of reasonably reliable contraceptive devices and abortion provide a means for keeping population and resources in balance. An important social consequence of these methods is that they are controlled increasingly by females.

Contemporary behavior and attitudes may suggest that the traditional biblically informed family relationship is less useful than in the past. The relationships of each individual to the larger society are more important than his or her relationship to the family. Older patterns for the regulation of sexuality made all forms of sexual activity taboo except those between married partners that were potentially procreative. Such of those admonitions which resulted in increased population are of substantially less value today.

Let us now turn to the major textual expression of the classical idea of marriage in Western civilization, the Bible.

NOTES

1. J. M. Tanner, "Sequence, tempo, and individual variation in growth and development of boys and girls aged twelve to sixteen." In Jerome Kagan and Robert Coles (eds.), *Twelve to Sixteen: Early Adolescence* (New York: W. W. Norton, 1972), pp. 1–24.
2. Adam Smith, *An Inquiry into the Nature and Causes of the Wealth of Nations,* ed. Edwin Cannan (New York: Modern Library, 1965), pp. 70–71. First published in 1776.

CHAPTER 3

The Centrality of Paternity[1]

As a first step in our deliberations it is important to recognize that the basic theme, and seeming preoccupation, of the Bible as a whole is paternity. I stress "first," because the burden of my argument will be to indicate that the Bible expresses certain profound and almost "unconscious" alternatives to this overall message. Paternity is the biological fact that men are necessary for the birth of a child. As a preoccupation of the Bible, paternity is the phenomenon around which the basic elements of biblical theology and social, political, and economic relationships are structured.

The awareness of the existence of a biological relationship between male consorts of women and the children of those women is the keystone of a social reality of family in the first place. Alternatively there are only such kinship structures as might be built out of mother-son, mother-daughter, and sibling-sibling ties.

Paternity is one of the most frequent themes in both the Old and the New Testaments. We can hardly open the Bible without finding some allusion to the biological connectedness between male progenitors and their offspring. So preoccupied were the authors of the Bible with fatherhood that even God is conceived of as father. This idea, we shall presently see, may have been understood more concretely and less metaphorically. We presume that the biblical authors projected onto God characteristics of their own that were of great moment to them. In other great historical works, such as those of Plato or Aristotle, paternity is referred to much less often, and, by contrast to the Bible, appears to be of less concern to the authors.

There is now considerable evidence that the composition of the first five or six books of the Bible, the Pentateuch or the Hexateuch, spanned many centuries. We may thus presume that the processes of family formation, in the sense of building social relations on the basis of the understanding of biological paternity, also spanned that time or longer. Indeed, it may well be that the project of accounting for the male's biological role in birth has been ongoing in social relations since the discovery of that scientific fact.

With perhaps some exception, it is most likely that the authorship of the Bible is male. This is the case if we accept the most traditional view, that the Bible was dictated by God to Moses and others, or the contemporary scholarly view that it is a compilation from the hands of J, E, D, P, etc. (as some of the presumptive authors emerging from documentary analysis are designated). It was unlikely that this set of books was written either by women or by people who were very young. It is, rather, the writing of people who were fathers, or at least potential fathers. It has recently been suggested that one possible exception is the *Song of Solomon,* which sometimes speaks in the first-person singular feminine. For example,"Let him kiss me with kisses of his mouth" (Song of Solomon 1:2)[2] might have had a female author.

The Bible may be interpreted as a document representing the crisis of paternalization, all the changes involved in the male's assumption of the various obligations of fatherhood. This crisis is not only associated with some historical period in which males took on the social status of fatherhood as a common expectation; it is also a crisis repeated in the individual life history of many males who become fathers. Historically, the composition of the biblical text corresponds to a period following the discovery of the role of the male in conception and simultaneous with the development of the patriarchal ideas of marriage and their social integration, especially the notion of fidelity. Within a life history the crisis of paternalization is repeated in each male who lives long enough to mature into the potential for, or actuality of, parenthood. It may well be that one reason for the continued acceptance of the Bible over history is due to its resonance with this crisis in generation after generation of males of our civilization.

If we take it that the Bible is part of the process whereby males involved themselves in the responsibilities of caring for children, then the Bible may also be regarded as expressing what may be considered the effeminization of the male. In coming to share the care of children, he came to share in the archaic function of the female. In coming to understand that he was biologically connected with children, he became like a mother. Indeed, even such super-masculine traits as are associated with being a warrior may be seen as outgrowths of a mother's protectiveness with respect to her children. In this sense, "paternalization" is equally "maternalization" of the male.

The biblical mind was profoundly aware that children could be created at will, as it were. Men were virtually, if not quite, gods in this respect. Sexual intercourse was euphemistically referred to as *knowledge,* for it touched on the ultimate knowledge of the creation of humanity. The Bible may, in part, be understood as an expression of the shock of men as they realized that they could be the willful creators of human beings, creators as they had imagined their gods to have been.

The biblical authors also ascribed to God what must have appeared a right matching that of creation: the right of destruction. "And YHWH was sorry that he had made the man on earth, and it grieved Him in his heart. And YHWH said, I will blot out the man whom I have created from on the face of the earth" (Genesis 6:6–7).

Creation and destruction are dialectically related and converge in will. The biblical mind thrilled over the awareness that a willful sexual act could result in the creation of a child. The human understanding of the power to create other human beings at will was joined to the awareness that the indefinite life of an individual was *not* a matter of will. The union of these two observations yielded the possibility of achieving biological immortality by willfully conceiving children. The biblical mind, however, endowed God with a trait that men did not have: immortality. The genius of the biblical mind perhaps expresses itself best in the Abraham narrative, in the detailed account of the Covenant (Genesis 15, 17). The Covenant entails a God to provide a land for Abraham's offspring to live on after Abraham's death, "a land flowing with milk and honey" (Exodus 3:8), that is, food suitable for young children. Thus, the Covenant was a kind of primitive life insurance policy, designed to provide for the children when the mortal father was gone. The identification of man with his offspring was, however, made difficult by several factors.

First, the offspring might not be loyal, might not continue to provide, might not continue to obey, and might even kill their parents. The strenuous obedience morality of the Bible is related to such possibilities. Indeed, the only one of the ten commandments that indicates a consequence is that of honoring one's father and mother, which is followed by "in order that your days may be extended on the earth" (Exodus 20:12), suggesting that, if parents are not honored, one's days on this earth might be shortened.

Second, the simple burden of raising children under shortages of resources was itself a threat.

The third difficulty was the possible lack of authentic paternity. The biblical mind had little difficulty in entertaining polygamy,[3] but polyandry was intolerable. The uncertainty was especially great about the first born, because the first born is ever of dubious paternity if the gestation period is not known. The Bible indeed suggests killing all first born—"sanctify unto me all the first born, whatsoever opens the womb among the children of Israel. . . . It is mine" (Exodus 13:2)—although the text also allows the exemption of the human first born by the payment of five silver shekels to the priest of the temple, a redemption (Numbers 18:15–16).

These difficulties arising from men's assuming responsibility for *their* children also gave rise to a temptation to kill their children. Infanticide is not rare either in Western history or in other cultures. A large part of the Bible's moral burden is to prevent infanticide from actually taking place. One interpretation of the story of the

Garden of Eden is that, since the tree was the tree of knowledge, the word for which also means copulation, the sin of eating the produce from that tree was the eating of one's own children. The covering of the genitalia following the eating also suggests that this might be the case; as does Eve's punishment of pain in having children, that she might be reminded that the produce of her knowledge was not to be eaten; and Adam's labor, his acceptance of the burden of providing for the continued maintenance of Eve and children. An essential feature of Judaism and Christianity is a binding of the father to not act out the impulse to kill the children and to provide the resources for the family's maintenance.

One of the main historical functions of the Judeo-Christian tradition has been to counteract the impulse toward infanticide or abandonment that may arise as a dialectical antithesis to men's assumption of paternal responsibility. The theme of infanticide is central to some of the most significant developments in Judaism and Christianity. Moses is saved from a holocaust of infant slaughter. Jesus is saved from a holocaust of infant slaughter. The great historical moment for Judaism in the biblical narrative is the almost-slaying of Isaac. The great historical moment for Christianity in the biblical narrative is the crucifixion of Jesus, said to be the son of God.

The temptation to kill children must have been real to have provoked the writers of the Bible to speak out against it. Ezekiel, for example, complained: "For when they had slaughtered their children in sacrifice to their idols, on the same day they came into my sanctuary to profane it" (Ezekiel 23:30). Isaiah scolded: "You relieve yourselves by the oaks, under every luxuriant tree, and slaughter the children in the valleys under the cracks of the rocks" (Isaiah 57:5). The prophets railed against idolatry, which was associated with the sacrifice of children; and against adultery and "whoredom," from which would arise unwanted children.

In the biblical text child sacrifice is often associated with the deity Molech, for example: "And do not give your seed over to Molech" (Leviticus 18:21). Since there are no vowels in biblical Hebrew, and the word might be read as Molech or Melech, the latter meaning king, one might read the commandment in Leviticus as "And do not give your seed over to the king." Reading Molech rather than Melech is a tendentious misvocalization, the vowels being taken from the word *boshet,* meaning shame, to give the meaning "shameful king." In the Judeo-Christian tradition the Messiah is the longed-for, awaited, royal, redeeming, charismatic descendant of David. This new king was to be a different kind of king, one who used his power not for slaying children but rather for their deliverance. The kingdom of God is antithetical to, and yet dialectically related to, kingdoms in which the king had the right to dispose of human life at will. Evidence that messianism was associated with royalty is reflected in the Gospel story of the ironic play of the soldiers with Jesus:

> And they clothed him in a purple cloak, and plaiting a crown of thorns they put it on him. And they began to salute him, "Hail, King of the Jews!" And they struck his head with a reed, and spat upon him, and they knelt down in homage to him. And when they had mocked him, they stripped him of the purple cloak, and put his own clothes on him. And they led him out to crucify him. (Mark 15:17–20, Revised Standard Version).

The very idea of the Messiah as a new kind of king must be understood in the context of biblical history. Following the death of Solomon, that history was stormy. Population pressure in the land was great, in contrast to nomadic conditions, when children are more assets than liabilities. Frequent reversions to the Molech tradition and its associated child sacrifice took place. Even Solomon built a high place for Molech (I Kings 11:7). Child sacrifice is variously alluded to (II Kings 16:3; 21:6; 23:10; II Chronicles 33:6; Jeremiah 7:31; 19:5; Ezekiel 16:20; 20:26). In contrast there was always the promise that contained the words of God to Abraham: "Because I will bless you very much and multiply your seed very much, as the stars of the heaven, and as the sand which is on the edge of the sea; and your seed will inherit the gate of his enemies" (Genesis 22:17).

In the messianic tradition, saving is being saved from slaughter in infancy. The Messiah is indeed the savior, saving the child from nonexistence. Messianic salvation of the child from the threat of nonexistence, I believe, underlies the ritual of baptism. Throughout human history drowning has been one of the most readily available ways of getting rid of unwanted children. Being saved from drowning is thus a paradigm for being saved from infanticide. In the story of Moses, Pharaoh condemns the children to death by drowning in the Nile. Moses was saved from death in the Nile, and, according to the explanation of the text, he was named by that act of salvation, (Exodus 2:1–10). Jesus is also "saved" from drowning, as it were. It is precisely at his baptism that Jesus' messiahship is revealed to him:

> In those days Jesus came from Nazareth of Galilee and was baptized by John in the Jordan. And when he came up out of the water, immediately he saw the heavens opened and the Spirit descending upon him like a dove; and a voice came from heaven, "Thou art my beloved Son; with thee I am well pleased." (Mark 1:9–11)

Coming out of the water—in my interpretation, being saved from drowning—Jesus receives an affirmation of his existence from the *father*. "Thou art my beloved Son; with thee I am well pleased." What is the alternative? I am not pleased with you, you are not my beloved son, and you may stay in the water!

Given its unique dependency, for the human infant to live there must be a second affirmation of existence, the assurance of long-term care and protection. It is not enough just to be born to have a claim upon existence. Being born is, of itself, merely the result of sexuality. One is born of original sin, and in jeopardy because of the sin of Adam, who ate the produce of the tree of knowledge. Within this tradition, baptism, as a second affirmation, by someone who will assume the responsibility of care, is regarded as essential. Not only is the child to be born, but someone must claim it; someone must acknowledge its right to live. There must be someone to draw it out of the water, as Moses was drawn out and as Jesus was drawn out. The baptism still retains its meaning in that the baptized are thus identified as belonging to the Church, as belonging to the extended human family that the Church represents. Infants who are baptized are pledged to the Church by their parents, and thereby the parents are pledged to the child. This historical association between the idea of baptism and the solidarity of the family and the Church reflects an essential meaning of baptism.

Circumcision is similarly the bearer of a complex of meanings. Some of the meanings of baptism are shared textually, if not historically, by the more ancient circumcision in Judaism. Circumcision is essentially an affirmation of the child's right to exist in the larger community, analogous to the Christian church. Circumcision differs from baptism in the method of killing the child which is alluded to. Whereas baptism recalls drowning, in circumcision it is being killed by a knife, possibly an allusion to the way Isaac might have been killed by Abraham. The Bible indicates that the eighth day after birth is the first permissible day for the sacrifice of animals (Leviticus 22:27) Circumcision is equally performed on the eighth day (Genesis 17:12).

Baptism and circumcision are both symbols of the sacrifice of the child. As symbols they are substitutes for the sacrifice, and in this way they are redemptive. They are then actually ceremonies of acceptance rather than of sacrifice.

These two ceremonies are associated with naming the child. In the history of civilization, name is very important. The right to a name is the right to life; the absence of a name is the absence of a right to life. Granting a child his name constitutes a pledge on the part of the father to care for that child. In the circumcision ceremony the child is granted not just one name but two names linked together. When Isaac receives a name at his circumcision, he is not called simply Isaac. He is called *Isaac, the son of Abraham.* Jesus is called *Jesus, the son of Joseph.* A social blood bond is established between father and son to remove all doubt of the existence of a prior biological blood bond. The ceremony is essentially a declaration on the part of the father similar to "Thou art my beloved son; with thee I am well pleased."

Dropping the ancient requirement of circumcision was clearly a way of easing entry into the Christian faith for Gentiles (Acts 15). The early Christian evidently took to heart the rabbinic distinction

between light and severe sins, the latter most notably idolatry, incest, and murder, not to be violated even on pain of death (BT
Nezikin: Sanhedrin 74a).[4] The early Christian leaders indicated that
it was only necessary "to abstain from the pollutions of idols and
from unchastity and from what is strangled and from blood" (Acts
15:20). Christianity sought to place the acceptance of people, their
deliverance, on a less contingent basis than acceptance by just one
particular man, the father. Indeed, one of the interesting features of
Acts is that, although in the fifteenth chapter we are informed of
the events associated with dropping the circumcision requirement,
the very next chapter tells the story of Paul's circumcising Timothy,
who, though the son of a Jewish mother, was the son of a Greek
father: "Paul wanted Timothy to accompany him; and he took him
and circumcised him because of the Jews that were in those places,
for they all knew that his father was a Greek" (Acts 16:3). Essentially, dropping circumcision as a requirement for admission to the
Christian Church constituted an affirmation of the right to life
independent of the kinship origins first associated with that right in
the biblical mind.

The Passover is of utmost importance in both Judaism and Chris-
tianity. For Judaism it commemorates the exodus from Egypt. For
Christianity it is the occasion of the Last Supper, the basis of the
Eucharist, in which Jesus' injunction of the Last Supper is regularly
carried out, and the foundation for deepening the communion of
Christians with Christ and each other.

The main feature of the historical event commemorated by the
Passover is the slaying and the sparing of children. Within the
biblical narrative it can be seen as Moses's delayed revenge on
Pharaoh for having killed the children of the Israelites at the time
of his own infancy, an instance of the biblical *lex talionis* (law of
retaliation—an eye-for-an-eye), the occasion for the death of Egyptian first born, and a harbinger of Herod's order to kill all the male
infants in Bethlehem in his effort to kill the infant Jesus (Matthew
2:16).

In preparation for slaying the first-born children of the Egyptians,
God commands:

let each man take a lamb. . . . The lamb shall be without blemish, a male, in the first year. . . . And the whole assembly of the congregation of Israel shall slaughter it at dusk. And they shall take from the blood and put it on the two door posts and on the lintel of the houses in which they will eat it. . . . And so should you eat it: your loins girded, your shoes on your feet, and your staffs in your hands, and you will eat it hurriedly—it is the Passover of YHWH. And I will pass over the land of Egypt in this night, and I will strike every first-born in the land of Egypt, from man to beast. . . . And the blood will be a sign of you in the houses where you are; and when I see the blood I will pass over you. And there will be no plague on you to destroy you when I strike in the land of Egypt. (Exodus 12:3–13)

Here we have as well the root story of Christianity. In the New Testament, Jesus is referred to as the paschal lamb—"For Christ, our paschal lamb, has been sacrificed" (I Corinthians 5:7)—and his blood is the blood of the lamb (Revelations 7:14). His sacrifice to the "father" is the means whereby others are saved from the expression of the infanticidal impulse. In the history of Christianity, the bloody cross is taken as a protection against evil, against the infanticidal impulse in my interpretation. Like the bloody door posts and lintel, the cross protects against evil and death. Where there is the sign of the cross, the bloody cross, the cross marked with the blood of the lamb, the cross made with the blood of Jesus, there the impulse against the first born will not come to rest. Jesus is the "lamb without blemish" (Hebrews 9:14).

We can understand the gospel accounts of the Last Supper as an injunction against the commission of infanticide in a context of about two thousand years in which virtually all evil was conceptualized in terms of the wrath and death-dealing of the father-god. The time of Jesus was a time of great poverty, and thus a time when the temptation to kill children would be great. Some, such as the Essenes, a fellowship that lasted from about the second century B.C. to the first century A.D., lived ascetic lives in communities without marriage or the presence of women. Jesus, of course, did not marry. Paul expressed his begrudging enthusiasm for marriage: ". . . It is well . . . to remain single as I do. But if they cannot exercise self-control, they should marry. For it is better to marry than to be aflame with passion" (I Corinthians 7:8–9). The conditions were ripe for infanticide as indeed we know was the case from the episode of Herod slaying the children of Bethlehem.[5]

Jesus preached the unreliability of earthly fathers: "And call no man your father on earth, for you have one Father, who is in heaven" (Matthew 23:9). He offered a haven in the comfort of a heavenly father for those who had failed or been failed by family life. "And every one who has left houses or brothers or sisters or father or mother or children or lands, for my name's sake, will receive a hundredfold, and inherit eternal life" (Matthew 19:29).

NOTES

1. Some of the thought in this chapter has been presented earlier in a chapter entitled "Paternity in the Judeo-Christian Tradition," in Alan W. Eister (ed.), *Changing Perspectives in the Scientific Study of Religion* (New York: John Wiley & Sons, 1974), pp. 203–216; and in Bakan, *The Duality of Human Existence* (Boston: Beacon Press, 1966).
2. I have made no effort to follow any translation from the Hebrew consistently. Although I have borrowed freely from available translations, thus claiming no originality in this respect, the translations from the Hebrew are my own. The Talmud says that anyone who translates literally is a liar, and anyone who modifies in translation is a blasphemer (BT, Nashim: Kiddushin 49a). In general, I have opted for the lie of literalness.
3. It should be pointed out that Jewish law subsequently, under the so-called Cherem of Rabbenu Gershom b. Judah, from the tenth and eleventh centuries, allowed the taking of an additional wife only with the approval of at least one hundred rabbis from three countries and allowed divorce only with the consent of the wife.
4. Hereafter throughout the book references from the Babylonian Talmud will be introduced by the letters BT.
5. Some related thoughts in connection with the phenomenon of child abuse may be found in Bakan, *Slaughter of the Innocents* (Boston: Beacon Press, 1973).

CHAPTER 4

A Frame for the Text

How shall we understand the dynamics and the development of this great protective transgenerational spirit called Abba, the Hebrew for father, and so even retained untranslated at times in Greek and English translations of the Bible (Mark 14:36, Romans 8:15; Galatians 4:6)?

In this chapter I will sketch, in the broadest of brush-strokes, with some details to be given in subsequent chapters, a developmental sequence which the study of the biblical text suggests to me. Let us start not with the beginning, not with the end, but with a critical middle stage in this presumptive sequence, represented by four verses from the sixth chapter of Genesis. These four verses have stood as a major puzzle for virtually all students of the Bible over the centuries, and there is still no consensus about their meaning. Indeed, the theme of these verses, the marriage between the "sons of God" and the "daughters of men" is, at least on the face of it, quite alien to any common understanding of the Bible's moral intention. It is from these verses that I have taken the title of this book because of my judgment of their critical importance in an understanding of the remainder of the biblical text.

(1) And it came to pass, when men began to multiply on the face of the earth, and daughters were born to them. (2) And the sons of God saw the daughters of men, that they were good; and they took themselves wives, whomsoever they chose. (3) And YHWH said: "My spirit shall

not abide in man forever, because he is flesh; and his days will be a hundred and twenty years." (4) The Nephilim were in the earth in those days, and also after that, when the sons of God came in to the daughters of men, and they bore children to them. The same were the valorous ones of old, the men of fame. (Genesis 6:1–4)

At this point in our consideration of this remarkable passage I would indicate only that the text allows the possibility of sexual relations between the "sons of God" and the "daughters of men," and that offspring may result from such unions. In our common understanding of the biblical text, a similar situation arises only in some interpretations of the birth of Jesus. I will presently try to show that the theme of divine impregnation, which is alluded to here, is of great significance throughout the biblical text.

What, one may well ask, is this amazing passage doing in this document? The Bible characteristically ascribes a *creative* role to the divine. Why is there here so blatant an indication of the sons of God as *procreative,* as sexually generative? Within the classical Jewish tradition even a hint of divine procreativity constitutes an obscenity. Why, if once written, did it escape censorship in the numerous editings over history?

Assuredly, the ascription of procreative powers to gods is not unusual in history. The idea of descent from gods was common enough in the ancient world. Thus, in Plato's *Timaeus,* ". . . and we must accept the traditions of the men of old time who affirm themselves to be the offspring of the gods—that is what they say— and they must surely have known their own ancestors. How can we doubt the word of the children of the gods?"[1] The Greek gods were allowed their sexual and procreative adventures. There are indications that Sumerian, Akkadian, Hittite, Ugaritic, and other gods engaged in sexual relations both among themselves and with mortals. Such tales also existed among the peoples of ancient Palestine. Royal claims of divine descent are ubiquitous in history. Until very recently it was still held that the Japanese royal family descended from the sun goddess Amaterasu and the storm god Susanowo.

Thus the theme of Genesis 6 is not historically extraordinary.

What is extraordinary is that it remained in the biblical text. For it is incompatible, at least on the surface, with what appears to be the spirit and the moral imperatives of the remainder of the text, and certainly with the norms of the cultures that were associated with the text. One explanation of the presence of this and some other material "offensive to later religious tastes" in *Genesis* is that some of the documents that were finally compiled into the text had early become so widely accepted as to be quasi-canonical, making the compilers hesitant to alter them.[2] My argument is that the presence of the story of the "sons of God" in the text is explained by reasons beyond such deference.

I suggest that the historical developmental sequence that the text represents requires the allusion to this theme as an arch requires its keystone. The idea of divine impregnation is a critical stage in the sequence. Without some such allusion to the theme of divine impregnation, the development would lack a major stage and the resulting beliefs and values would be less credible.

There is at least heuristic value in thinking about development as taking place in stages. Each stage in a developmental sequence is the aim of earlier stages and the precondition for subsequent stages. Moreover, earlier stages in a developmental sequence never disappear entirely but continue to exist, at least in some form. In psychoanalytic thought the preexistent stages are regarded as abiding in the "unconscious" as traces of the past. More concretely this means that, although explicit manifestations associated with preexistent stages may not be evident, they may manifest themselves at any time. The psychoanalytic conceptualization of abiding existence in an unconscious may be questioned, but the reality of abiding existence itself is unquestionable, and it is to the credit of the psychoanalytic school of thought to have identified the phenomenon. In this book I assume the abiding existence of earlier developmental stages of human culture. At the same time I am fully aware that such a developmental sequence may be only a rough approximation of the reality.

Consider four prevalent human concerns: *origin, death, property,* and *power.* These constitute major preoccupations of the biblical authors. Indeed, the greatness of the Bible lies precisely in the aptness with which these abiding human concerns are addressed by the authors.

Now note that all four of these concerns are addressed in the four verses of Genesis. The verses indicate the *origin* of the men of valor. They indicate that life is terminal; although *death* comes only after a generous 120 years of life. They indicate prerogative of use, the essence of *property,* with respect to the daughters of men for the sons of God, who take whomsoever they chose. They indicate that the men who emerged from these matings were men of *power.*

The text suggests the following set of developmental stages, bearing on marriage and family:

1. An initial stage of total ignorance concerning the role of the male in procreation, and in which, if lineage has any meaning at all, there is only matrilineality. That women have babies is empirically obvious. However, the role of the male in conception and childbirth is a matter of inference, "scientific discovery," as it were.

There has been debate among anthropologists about primitive people's awareness of the relationship between sexual intercourse and childbirth. For example, there have been challenges to Malinowski's claim that the Trobriand Islanders were not privy to this information.[3] However, the anthropological data are irrelevant here. A priori, there must have been a time, whenever it was, when this discovery had not yet been made. Ancient people cannot uncritically be identified with contemporary people studied by anthropologists. In any case, awareness of the role of the male in conception is evident in the biblical text. The text as a whole may be interpreted as reflecting the effort to integrate this piece of information into a world view.

2. The emergence of the sense of the mystery of conception. There is the obvious fact that women are sometimes pregnant and sometimes not pregnant. But why? There must have been a time in history when conception was a mystery, a question and a wonder. Whenever mystery arises, humans almost universally begin to resolve it by explaining it in terms of divine will. Thus at this stage

the theory emerges that conception is the result of divine action. The relationship of sex to procreation is not yet perceived.

3. Next the great scientific discovery that conception results from sexual intercourse between a male and a female is made.

4. The conflict between the ideas of stage 2 and stage 3 is perhaps the most classical form of "warfare of science with theology," similar to the warfare that followed the publication of Darwin's *On the Origin of Species*.[4] Both conflicts concerned two explanations of the origin of humanity—one divine and the other scientific.

One convenient way to resolve the inconsistency between conception as a result of divine intervention, on the one hand, and conception as a result of sexual intercourse, on the other, is to attribute sexuality to the divine. The two notions are easily compatible if one accepts the idea that gods are sexual beings who may impregnate earthly women. Pregnancy thus results from both divine intervention and sexual intercourse. This resolution has the interesting consequence that it continues to allow earthly lineage to be matrilineal, and allowing the belief of divine descent. The verses cited, Genesis 6:1–4, should be understood as belonging to this stage.

5. However, this solution is far from fully satisfactory, especially for males. For them the scientific discovery had the overwhelming consequence that they could create—procreate—human beings at will, whereas before it was thought that the gods did it! An ideological position was necessary to legitimate the prerogatives the great discovery appeared to allow them. Such legitimacy could result from firmly distinguishing between *create* and *procreate,* allowing the former to the divine while reserving the latter to men. This distinction is clearly contained in the biblical text.

6. The next stage is to replace matrilineal with patrilineal descent. A major metaphorical device, found in the text, is to conceptualize the male sexual exudate as "seed." This way of thinking attributes all the genetic endowment to the male and none to the female.

7. Guaranteed paternal authenticity is now required. If the seed is that of the male, if it is his property, then it is essential to develop social methods of guaranteeing female fidelity in marriage and vir-

ginity prior to marriage. Such female "purity" guarantees that the offspring of the female are the offspring of the male.

8. But how can one develop the authority, the power, to guarantee sexual fidelity and virginity? At the next stage, this authority is attributed to the divine.

9. As for the male, he assumes obligations of maintenance, protection, and education of the offspring, which have, prior to that, been associated with the female. With these obligations he assumes the power to provide them. He becomes a man of strength and valor, a man of arms. He takes on the primitive maternal cub-protecting traits, which become the marks of masculinity.

10. While masculine pride as hero-provider, hero-protector, and hero-teacher is associated with these obligations, the male also thus becomes "effeminized" at the same time, for to become a father, with all of its ramifications, means that the male must also become a "mother" to the children. Paternity consists in the male's assumption of previously maternal obligations to children. For primitive femaleness consists precisely in providing maintenance, protection, and education to the young.

11. With the male effeminized, a new theological possibility is opened up: The relationship of a male to the god shall be as that of a wife to the husband. This requires first that the god must be a *single* god, analogous to the single husband of the wife; the religion thus must be monolatrous. Secondly, the male's fidelity to the god shall be as wife to husband. With such a theological view, the moral imperatives addressed to the female can be presented in the rhetoric of fidelity to god. And a husband's jealousy is legitimated in an image of a jealous god.

12. The idea of fidelity, both as fidelity of man to god and fidelity of wife to husband, could be extended one step further, to fidelity of man to lord or king, especially if an association of king as father and king as divine could be made credible. This inference was certainly drawn from the Bible throughout postbiblical history by aristocracy and royalty.

NOTES

1. *The Dialogues of Plato,* Vol. II, tr. B. Jowett (New York: Random House, 1937), p. 22.
2. Yehezkel Kaufmann, *The Religion of Israel,* tr. and abridged by Moshe Greenberg (New York: Schocken Books, 1972), pp. 208–210.
3. See Bronislaw Malinowski, *The Father in Primitive Psychology* (New York: W. W. Norton, 1966).
4. See the one-time widely read book by Cornell University's first president, Andrew Dickson White, *A History of the Warfare of Science with Theology in Christendom* (London: Macmillan and Co., 1896).

CHAPTER 5

Background

In this chapter let us review some information concerning the biblical text itself. The Old Testament, which received this name on the basis of the writings of Paul,[1] characteristically designated as Law, Prophets, and Writings in the Hebrew canon, developed over about a thousand years, from about 1200 to 100 B.C. Around 100 A.D. a synod of rabbis gathered at Jabneh, a center of Jewish intellectual life at the time. This synod, recognizing the threat to the classical Jewish heritage from both syncretistic apocalyptic movements within Judaism and the new Christianity, fixed the canon of sacred scriptures. What had been gradually developing was declared binding. Judaism, it was hoped, could clearly identify its own scriptural sources against others.[2]

THE PROCESS OF COMPOSITION

The Bible is the product of a multitude of hands, and each hand that wrote was informed by many mouths that spoke. Much of what was eventually written was subject to precise memorization and recitation. Much of what was first set down was subject to many editings and deliberate and nondeliberate changes in the hand copying that preceded the Gutenberg technology of the fifteenth century. However, the preserved biblical scrolls from the Dead Sea first discovered in 1947, said to be considerably older than manuscripts previously available, have indicated that the copying errors were far less than some had suspected. Much of what was actually written down in the Hebrew text was only a form of shorthand, in the sense that the meaning could be extracted only by knowledge of an orally transmitted vocalization with vowels and consonants, the written text having been exclusively consonantal. It was not until the end of the first millennium A.D. that vowels were included in the codexes used for study. The scrolls used for the public reading are even to this day written without the vowel signs.

The composers of the text drew heavily on speeches, sermons, prayers, contracts, letters, lists, laws, cultic ordinances, myths, fairy tales, fables, tales, sagas, legends, reports, popular histories, autobiographies, accounts of dreams and visions, prophetic autobiographies, poems, sayings, proverbs, riddles, numerous songs of work and harvest, drinking songs, songs of marriage and love, watchman's songs, mocking songs, funeral dirges, royal songs, victory songs, cultic songs, spiritual songs, and poems of instruction.[3]

Yet, at the same time, the Bible is not simply a collection of remnants of ancient works. We should not consider the written words as completely original, yet we should not discount authorship completely. It is helpful in this light to compare more recent contributions to other world literature. Shakespeare, as we know, built many of his plays on available stories. Goethe's great epic, *Faust,* was based on various versions of the Faust legend that go back at least to Augustine's encounter in the fourth century with "a certain Bishop of the Manichees, Faustus by name, a great snare of the Devil."[4]

Various types of archeological materials bear on the way we may regard the Bible. The Bible relates to history first as a record of the history of the world prior to the Christian era, and secondly as a profoundly important item in the history of the world since its composition. Archeological materials continue to be discovered that bear on both aspects of the Bible.

The essential elements of the creation story as told in the Bible are to be found in the Babylonian epic *Enuma Elish,* which existed in the twenty-second century B.C. The story of the flood as told to

Gilgamesh by Utnapishtim in the Gilgamesh Epic, which came to the Babylonians from the earlier Sumerian civilization, and the flood story in the Babylonian Atrakhasis Epic, both of which are available to us on clay tablets from ancient times, are undoubtedly related to the biblical story of Noah and the flood.

In the Louvre in Paris there is a piece of carved black diorite from the time of the rule of Hammurabi of Babylon, in the eighteenth century B.C. This is several centuries before the birth of Moses, which, if we consider the biblical chronology, would have been around the thirteenth century B.C. Carved into the stone is a detailed record of almost three hundred legal decisions by Hammurabi on commerce, marriage and divorce, crime, and civil obligations. The discovery of this record by Jean-Vincent Scheil, a French Orientalist, at the beginning of the twentieth century shocked the religious world, for there is a remarkable resemblance between the laws of Hammurabi and the laws of Moses. It remains an open question as to whether the laws of Moses came from the Code of Hammurabi, or whether both drew from a common heritage that was even more ancient. There are now excavated collections of laws, Ur-Nammu, Eshrunna, and Lipit-Ishtar, from 2050 to 1850 B.C. similar to and antedating even the Code of Hammurabi. There can be little question that the law expressed in the Bible must be far more ancient than we are led to believe by the biblical narrative.

Lack of direct archeological evidence to confirm a Hebrew presence in Egypt has been disturbing to some scholars. Harry M. Orlinsky, for example, attempts to explain this lack in terms of the Egyptian humiliation at the hands of the Hyksos, who conquered Egypt in 1720 B.C. and dominated it until 1550 B.C.: "For the Egyptians themselves, humiliated by their conquest at the hands of the Hyksos, avoided and suppressed any reference to the events of the period, and it would have been well-nigh impossible for anyone to learn the historical details very much later."[5] Some have speculated that the ancient Hebrews are the Habiru variously mentioned in Near Eastern documents from about the twentieth to the twelfth centuries B.C. But at best the Hebrews would have been but one of several groups of people called Habiru.[6] Much more disturbing with respect to the biblical story of a Hebrew presence in Egypt is the Mernaptah Stele from Thebes, which dates from 1230 B.C. It contains the only known use of the word *Israel* to be found in ancient Egyptian documents, and, together with the early mention of the tribe of Asher in Egyptian documents, "raises the question of a possible Hebrew presence in Canaan before Joshua's conquest,"[7] a possibility quite at variance with the biblical narrative.

AUTHORSHIP OF THE PENTATEUCH

The deepest mystery concerning the authorship of the Bible is in connection with Torah, the Pentateuch, the first five books of the Bible. Tradition has named Moses as the receiver of the Torah from God. In the first chapter of *Joshua,* which comes immediately after Deuteronomy, Joshua is enjoined by God to follow the Torah that Moses commanded (Joshua 1:7). It is called the "Book of the Torah" (1:8), or the "Book of the Torah of Moses" (8:31). In other parts of the Bible, including the New Testament, Moses and the Pentateuch are also linked. The traditional view of the Pentateuch is that it is a singular revealed document; its origin was divine and it was given to Moses, who then handed it down. "The Lord spoke to Moses face to face as a man speaks to a friend" (Exodus 33:11) and "mouth to mouth" (Numbers 12:8). Moses acted as a secretary or scribe taking dictation, writing down both the narrative portions and the commandments, though with tears in his eyes (BT, Kodashim: Menahoth 30a). The traditional view is expressed in the eighth of Maimonides's thirteen Principles of Faith, "I firmly believe that the whole Torah which is found now in our hands, is the one which was given to Moses, our teacher, may he rest in peace," which is regularly recited in the daily prayer. The Talmud does, however, recognize a problem in connection with the last few verses of the Pentateuch describing the death, burial, and mourning for Moses. Thus the Talmudic view is that Moses wrote the whole of the Pentateuch except the last eight verses, which were written by Joshua (BT, Nezikin: Baba Bathra, 14b; Kodashim: Menahoth 30a).

However, even the Talmud allows that there may be difficulties in connection with the authorship of the Pentateuch, as well as other books of the Old Testament. In a discussion of the question of authorship the Talmud says:

> Who wrote the Scriptures?—Moses wrote his own book[11] and the portion of Balaam and Job. Joshua wrote the book which bears his name and [the last] eight verses of the Pentateuch. Samuel wrote the book which bears his name and the Book of Judges and Ruth. David wrote the Book of Psalms, including in it the work of the elders, namely, Adam, Melchizedek, Abraham, Moses, Heman, Yeduthun, Asaph and the three sons of Korah. Jeremiah wrote the book which bears his name, the Book of Kings, and Lamentations. Hezekiah and his colleagues wrote Isaiah, Proverbs, the Song of Songs and Ecclesiastes. The Men of the Great Assembly wrote Ezekiel, the Twelve Minor Prophets, Daniel and the Scroll of Esther. Ezra wrote the book that bears his name and the genealogies of the Book of Chronicles up to his own time. (BT, Nezikin: Baba Bathra 14b–15a)[12]

There is also the question of whether the Torah was transmitted piecemeal or as a whole (BT, Nashim: Gittin 60a–60b). We find the Talmud indicating that certain sections were given to Moses on separate rolls on the day the Tabernacle was set up. The first of eight such presumptive scrolls is called "the section of priests," perhaps corresponding to Leviticus 17–26, which contemporary scholars refer to as the Holiness Code.

Various objections to Moses as author have been raised throughout history. For instance, Moses would not have represented God as swearing, Noah as drunk, Abraham with three wives. Nor would there be such repetitions or contradictions as are present in the text if Moses were author of it all. Thomas Hobbes, in *Leviathan,* stated that different parts of the Bible were written at different times. Spinoza accepted the view that Ezra was the compiler of the text and that the literary imperfections were due to the fact that Ezra did not complete his massive editorial job.

The development of the contemporary documentary hypothesis began in 1753, with the publication of *Conjectures sur les mémoires dont il paroit que Moyse s'est servi, pour composer le livre de la Genèse [Conjectures on the original memoirs which Moses seems to have used in composing the Book of Genesis]*. Published anonymously in Brussels, the book was written by Jean Astruc, a professor of medicine in Paris and personal physician to Louis XV. The work of Astruc follows the Enlightenment tendency to confront authority with empirical methods. Though still accepting authorship by Moses, Astruc developed the idea that Moses had several older documents before him as he wrote. Observation of the two names of God in text, Elohim and YHWH, led Astruc to speculate that Moses drew on two major, and a number of minor, documents.

Progress in disentangling the sources and documents that were compiled into the text followed. The hypothesis of Astruc was studied further by others. J. G. Eichhorn and K. D. Ilgen in the eighteenth century identified two different documents using Elohim; the "double Elohist" idea was further developed by H. Hupfeld in a book published in 1853. In 1805 M. L. De Wette identified the Book of Deuteronomy as that used in the reformation under King Josiah reported in II Kings 22–23. In 1878 Julius Wellhausen made a major contribution by identifying the "earlier Elohist" as a priestly writer, whom he designated as P, and demonstrating that this source had arisen after the exile. Wellhausen posited that the historical sequence was first J, the document using YHWH for the name of God; then E, the "later Elohist"; then D, the Book of Deuteronomy of King Josiah; and then P, a postexilic priestly hand.[13]

The nineteenth and twentieth centuries have enlarged our understanding of the text with archeological discoveries. Some six hundred sites in the biblical lands have been excavated. The Babylonian Creation Epic; the Gilgamesh Epic; the Code of Hammurabi; the Tell el Amarna tablets; inscriptions from Assyria, Egypt, and Persia; papyri from the fifth-century B.C. Jewish colony at Elephantine Island; the recovery of the languages of the Hittites and from the North Canaanite kingdom of Ugarit; cuneiform texts from the kingdoms of Mari on the Euphrates and Alah in Syria; the Dead Sea Scrolls; and other finds have considerably enriched our knowledge of the historical cultures associated with the text.

Although critics still disagree on the precise separation of the documents, there is general agreement among those who accept the documentary hypothesis that the narrative portion of the Pentateuch may be divided up into four major sources: The J (YHWH) document, composed in Jerusalem around 950 to 850 B.C.; the E (Elohim) document, composed around 750 B.C. by a priest in northern Israel; the D (Deuteronomy) document written by a priest in Jerusalem shortly before its discovery in 622 B.C.; and the P (Priestly) document, written by a priest around 450 B.C.

An important addition to the major documentary hypothesis is the division of the J document into J$_1$ and J$_2$, developed by Smend[14] and elaborated on by Simpson.[15] Simpson conceives of J$_2$ as having the J$_1$ document before him and making changes in it. R. H. Pfeiffer has advanced the notion that there is another document, which he calls S, that includes the odd fourteenth chapter of Genesis, in which Abram (Abraham) is depicted as a warrior, leading an army of 318 trained men (Genesis 14:14). According to Pfeiffer, S comes from another author living in Jerusalem around the time of J.[16]

THE HISTORICAL CONTEXT OF THE BIBLE'S COMPOSITION

The Bible was composed amid great political, social, economic, and military turbulence. The land in which the text was developed lay as a corridor within the Fertile Crescent, as it was named by James Henry Breasted, between Egypt to the west, and Assyria and Babylonia to the east, civilizations older than that of ancient Palestine. That the land experienced a great immigration of peoples in about the thirteenth century B.C. appears to have historical credibility. But whether that history is precisely the way it is recorded in the Bible is subject to doubt. Aside from its historical truth, however, a saga of immigration such as we find in the text was certainly important to the people of that land from the establishment of the kingdom under David and Solomon in the late eleventh and tenth centuries B.C. onward.

Before the establishment of the kingdom, the disunited peoples were subject to attack by marauders from the wilderness and by the Philistines to the west. The possession of technology for making iron weapons made the Philistines very formidable enemies.

The disunity among the other occupants of the land made them vulnerable. Around 1020 B.C. they united under Saul. Saul raised an army, defended Jabesh-Gilead against the Ammonites, and was subsequently acclaimed as king by a large part of the people (I Samuel 11:1 ff.). Saul was subsequently defeated in a battle at Mt. Gilboa (I Samuel 31) and committed suicide.

David became king of Judah, to the south, around 1010 B.C., and the king of all Israel around 1000 B.C., reigning for about half a century. He united the kingdom. He recovered the ark from the Philistines who had earlier captured it. He established a system of administration. He set Jerusalem as the capital. He established the Jewish "church" and forms of worship.

David sought to establish a dynasty. The text records that YHWH appears to Nathan with a message for David, promising him a dynasty: "When your days have been fulfilled, and you sleep with your fathers, I will set up your seed after you which issue from your bowels, and I will establish his kingdom. He will build a house for my name, and I will establish the seat of his kingdom forever" (II Samuel 7:12–13). This is virtually identical to YHWH's promise to Abraham, "he that issues from within your bowels will inherit from you" (Genesis 15:4). If we accept the scholarly opinion that the story of Abraham as we know it was written down after the establishment of the kingdom by David, we may entertain the possibility that the Abraham narrative was informed by the events associated with the establishment of the dynasty and served as a confirmation of the divine nature of the kingdom.

Solomon succeeded David and reigned for almost forty years, a period that was characterized by peace, which is, indeed, what Solomon's name means. The adjoining kingdoms of the Fertile Crescent were in relatively weakened condition. Solomon established treaties with several states, sealing them with numerous marriages. He developed chariot warfare, and sea and camel caravan transportation. He developed copper mining and smelting. He brought in skilled labor from other lands. He imported timber and gold and exported wheat and oil. He improved the system of administration. He developed a system of taxation and tribute. His huge building program included a temple to YHWH as well as buildings for the worship of other gods, such as Molech and Chemosh.

Soon after the death of Solomon the northern kingdom seceded, forming itself into the state of Israel, separate from the southern kingdom of Judah. New sanctuaries were built in the north at Bethel and Dan for the worship of golden calves (I Kings 12:28–33). Whatever the historical truth of the biblical story of the worship of the golden calf (Exodus 32) in the wilderness following the exodus, the presence of the story in the text may constitute an allusion to, and criticism of, the religious practices of the north.

The secession was followed by about two centuries of alternating periods of conflict and friendship between the north and the south and cycles of the rise and fall of power among the two kingdoms and the neighboring states. In the eighth century the power of Assyria under Tiglath-Pileser III grew and became threatening. The northern kingdom sought to develop alliances among the neighboring states against Assyria. When Judah refused to join, Israel proceeded against Judah to force its cooperation. Judah appealed for help from Assyria.

Tiglath-Pileser III conquered numerous cities of the north and transported large numbers of captives to Assyria in 733 B.C. His successor, Shalmaneser V, besieged Israel's capital for three years. It fell to his successor, Sargon II, in 721 B.C. Judah became a vassal state to Assyria. The "Assyrian system" entailed deporting residents and sending settlers from other parts of the Assyrian empire to Israel. Thus many of the northern inhabitants were carried off, forming the first exile. The exiles were absorbed into the Assyrian culture, giving rise to the idea of the ten lost tribes of Israel. The text says "there was none left but the tribe of Judah only" (II Kings 17:18). The northerners became the mixed-lineage Samaritans referred to in the text.

The threats to religious identity from the Assyrian dominion and the rise of pagan rites and rituals produced an intense counterreaction that eventually led to the great religious reform under King Josiah of Judah, who reigned from 640 to 609 B.C. During this period the power of the Assyrian empire was in decline.

During Josiah's reign a scribe named Shaphan found a roll of manuscript while repairs were being made in the Temple in 622 B.C. (II Kings 22:3–13; II Chronicles 35:15). He took it to Hilkiah, the priest, and the priest took it to the king. The Book of Deuteronomy has long been identified with this book of Josiah. The book was canonized as the word of God—the first book to be so canonized—and was adopted by Josiah as the basic law of the state of Judah. All other temples were destroyed, and all the pagan remnants in the Temple were removed.

Josiah was killed in battle with the Egyptians, who were allies of the Assyrians at the time. In the subsequent years Judah's power declined relative to the growing power of the new Babylonian empire under Nebuchadnezzar. In 597 B.C. Jehoiachin surrendered Jerusalem to Nebuchadnezzar, and all the royal family, warriors, leaders, craftsmen, and smiths were deported to Babylon. In response to a subsequent rebellion under Nebuchadnezzar's own appointee, Zedekiah, Nebuchadnezzar besieged and finally captured Jerusalem again in 587 B.C. He destroyed the Temple and the city and deported the entire remaining population except "the poorest of the land" (II Kings 25:12) to Babylon. This constituted the second exile.

The reactions to this second exile constitute the bulk of the Old Testament books of Zephaniah, Nahum, Habbakuk, Jeremiah, Ezekiel, and chapters 40–55 of the book of Isaiah (commonly called Deutero-Isaiah). In contrast to the cultural dissolution that took place as a result of the first exile of the northern kingdom, the victims of the second exile strenuously struggled to maintain the religion of YHWH and their cultural identity. They interpreted their disaster as divine punishment for disobedience. They codified the Temple laws and developed a system of synagogue worship to substitute for the Temple. They placed a renewed emphasis on the circumcision and the observance of the Sabbath—which served as a weekly reaffirmation of their communal identity—and developed a horror of intermarriage. The written text became extremely important, and they began the task of compiling other works that eventually entered the canon.

In 539 B.C. Cyrus II, the founder of the Persian Empire, conquered Babylon. He permitted the exiles that were still alive, and their descendants, to return to Judah, where they rebuilt the Temple and vigorously reinstituted worship of YHWH, nourished by the intense religious passion developed during the exile. The Temple was completed in 516 B.C. The rebuilding of the city was undertaken in 444 B.C. by Nehemiah, a descendant of those who had not immediately returned when Cyrus II released them from Babylon. Nehemiah was extremely wealthy and was influential in Persia, being the king's cupbearer. He persuaded the Persian King Artaxerxes to appoint him governor and to help him obtain the materials needed for the reconstruction. Over considerable opposition, especially from the Samaritans, and at the cost of impoverishment, inflation, and increased interest rates, the walls of Jerusalem were rebuilt.

Nehemiah, together with Ezra, a priest, bitterly opposed intermarriage, referring to it as a sin on the part of Solomon, who was made to sin by foreign women (Nehemiah 13:26). He expelled all aliens because it was "found written, that an Ammonite and a Moabite should not enter into the assembly of God for ever . . . in the book of Moses" (Nehemiah 13:1). Ezra ordered all the people to gather in Jerusalem on pain of forfeiting all property and banishment. Men who had married non-Jewish women were forced to divorce them (Ezra 10:1 ff.).

Nehemiah rebuilt the priesthood, which had fallen into poverty, by reforming the tithe system. Under Nehemiah's governance, all the people were gathered. Ezra mounted a pulpit that had been built for the purpose and read: "And they read in the book of the Torah of God distinctly; and they gave the meaning, and made them understand the reading" (Nehemiah 8:8). The Torah was declared the law of the commonwealth. It elicited great interpretative activities, leading to the development of the oral law, the Mishnah. Under Nehemiah and Ezra the program of tithes, sabbath, circumcision, festival observance, avoidance of intermarriage, and the learning of the Torah of Moses were vigorously enforced.

Tension was great between the returnees from the Babylonian exile and the northern Samaritans, the latter being the descendants of the older northern Israelites who intermarried with the Assyrian settlers sent there in the eighth century. The Samaritans were refused a role in the rebuilding of the Temple. The passionate Babylonian returnees were adamant against intermarriage with the Samaritans, and they expelled wives and children from such inter-marriages. It is in this period following the return from Babylon that the P document was presumably composed. Aramaic became the official language of the Persian Empire in this century, and it soon became the spoken language of the people in Palestine. Indeed, from this period onward the Hebrew language declined as a spoken lan-guage among Jews until it was reinstituted in modern Israel.

The conquest of Palestine by Alexander in 332 B.C. opened a new era. Palestine became a part of Hellenistically controlled Egypt. The Hellenistic period was characterized by the spread of Judaism throughout the empire in terms of births, travel, and extensive proselytizing, on the one hand; and by the cultural Hellenization of the Jews, on the other. There were at least four million Jews outside Palestine, dispersed through Egypt, Babylonia, Syria, and Asia Mi-nor around the beginning of the Christian Era, with Jews constitut-ing about a tenth of the population of the whole Mediterranean area. Synagogues were built all through the Hellenistic empire. There were twenty-eight Greek cities in Palestine. Greek became the com-mon language, and the Septuagint, the Greek translation of the Hebrew text, was the common Bible for the Jews. For example, Philo, for all his contribution to the study of the Bible, based his commentary exclusively on this Greek translation, and there is doubt that his knowledge of Hebrew was more than minimal. With-in Palestine there was often great cultural polarization, with the wealthier Jews characteristically leaning toward the Hellenistic norms away from the traditional Judaism of the time. In the early second century the priesthood was controlled by Hellenizing wealthy Jews. The status of the growing oral law became a major issue, with the Pharisees supporting the legal status of the oral law and the Sadducees accepting only the authority of the Torah itself.

After Pompey entered Jerusalem in 63 A.D. to quell a civil war, Palestine came under the dominion of Rome. Several unsuccessful

Jewish rebellions against Rome took place. The Temple, which had been rebuilt by Herod, was destroyed by the Romans in 70 A.D. The disaster at Masada took place in 73 A.D. An uprising led by Bar Kochba and Rabbi Akiva was ended in 135 A.D. From that time onward the Jews retired to a less militant and less rebellious posture, enjoying the right to internal rabbinic control in accordance with the Torah and the oral Torah. The Roman-dominated patriarchs— Gamaliel, who reigned from 135 to 175 A.D., and his son and successor Judah, called Judah the Prince, who reigned from 175 to 220 A.D.—invigorated and established the authority of the oral law. Under Judah the Mishnah was collected; subsequently the Talmud, as commentary on the Mishnah, developed.

TEXTS

No identifiable original manuscript of any part of the Bible has been discovered to date; every known extant manuscript is a copy of some preexisting document. Accounts of the original writing are to be found, however. For example, Jeremiah 36 provides an account of how Jeremiah dictated to Baruch, how Baruch read the book at the gate of the Temple and later to the princes, how the book was read to the King and destroyed, and how the book was rewritten. Many portions of the text were transmitted orally and learned "by heart." "And let these words which I command you this day be on your heart. And repeat them to your children, and speak them when you sit in your house and walk on the road and when you lie down and get up" (Deuteronomy 6:6–8) indicates an intense memorization program. Certainly the Mishnah, the oral law, which was finally organized in written form by Judah the Prince, was the object of such a memorization program. Indeed, the word *Mishnah* comes from the Hebrew word, *shanah,* which means to repeat. The fact that Hebrew ceased to be a spoken language around the third century B.C. may have been a determining factor in the development of the written text to preserve it.

Fragments from early periods exist. Qumran has yielded great treasures from very early periods, perhaps from the first century.

Qumran has yielded a piece of Greek translation and fragments in Hebrew that appear close to the Septuagint. The Nash Papyrus, now in Cambridge, England, containing the ten commandments and the "Hear, O Israel ..." (Deuteronomy 6:4) has been identified as coming from around the first century B.C. There are fragments from the sixth century A.D. from the storeroom of the old Cairo Synagogue. There are approximately a thousand extant manuscripts, of reasonable length, most of which come from the twelfth to fourteenth centuries A.D. Hardly any two comparable manuscripts agree in every detail. Indeed, it can be said that there was no standard edition of any part or version of the Bible until perhaps the first pages were pulled from the printing press; and some scholars, such as Harry Orlinsky, have said that there simply is no standard Hebrew text at all.

Until 1488, when the first printed edition of the Old Testament Hebrew was issued, and 1522, when the first printed edition of the Septuagint was issued, all versions were copied singly by hand. Indeed, not until the early nineteenth century did a standard pattern of 248 columns of 42 lines for copying a Torah scroll become established. The Masoretes, working from the sixth to the tenth centuries in Babylonia and Palestine, developed a complex apparatus for accurate copying. They counted letters, made determinations of middle letters so that the text could be checked by counting forward and backward, made checklists of biblical forms, and counted and recorded the occurrence of thousands of biblical words.

The oldest complete extant manuscript of the Old Testament in Hebrew is one dated 1009, located in the public library in Leningrad, designated as B19A. A printed version of it, with elaborate notes comparing it with other manuscripts by the editors, is available.[17]

Prior to the seventh century A.D. the written text was consonantal. Vowels and cantillation marks were added by the Masoretes between the seventh and ninth centuries A.D. Because of this, from ancient times through around the seventh century, the Hebrew text remained dependent upon an orally transmitted, repeatedly memorized, tradition. The absence of vowels in the classical texts made considerable memorization essential. In a sense, the written text

without the vowels was only an aid to memory, especially when
Hebrew was no longer a spoken language.

The absence of vowels is particularly significant in the meanings
of a number of passages. There are numerous examples where a
change in the vowels can change the meaning of a passage quite
dramatically. An example of this can be found in Amos 2:1. The
Jewish Publication Society translation, based on the vowels in the
standard text reads:

> Thus saith the Lord:
> For three transgressions of Moab,
> Yea, for four, I will not reverse it:
> Because he burned the bones of the king of Edom into lime.

W. F. Albright, building on the proposal of H. Tur-Sinai, suggests that it is far more meaningful to repoint the text (that is, to
add vowels) so that it reads:

> Thus Yahweh has spoken,
> Because of three offences of Moab,
> Because of four, I shall surely requite him!
> Because he burns the bones
> . . . of a human sacrifice to a demon.[18]

If Tur-Sinai and Albright have indeed recovered an earlier meaning, it is evident that the vowels that had been added had the effect
of removing an allusion to human sacrifice, which may have been
considered too odious to allow.

The cantillation marks added even later also can make a difference
in meaning. Rashi, the most distinguished of the rabbinic commentators, ascribed great importance to the cantillation marks as an aid
in finding the meaning in the text. For example, he refers to Ezekiel
1:11: "Had I not seen the accent [mark] . . . on the word . . . I would
not have been able to explain it."

The manuscripts of the Masoretes contain within themselves
several indications of the intrinsic problem of textual reliability.
There is the presence of the inverted *nun* (the letter N) in several
places to signal incorrect position or inauthenticity.[19] In ten places

there are dots over words, which the rabbinical tradition took to indicate doubtful passages. Dotting doubtful passages was an ancient practice for Greek manuscripts as well.[20] And perhaps most important are extensive indications in the margins of manuscripts instructing the reader to read the text differently from the text itself. There are some 1500 such indications. Some of the reading instructions are clearly intended to avoid blasphemy, such as the instruction to say Adonai where YHWH is written. Others are evidently intended to avoid obscenity, such as the instruction to say SHCHaV (lie with) for SHaGeL (coitus).[21] Gordis has argued that, for the most part, these reading instructions represent variant forms from other manuscripts. In several places, for example, the Isaiah manuscript from Qumran correspond to the later marginal instructions rather than the text of later manuscripts. The Septuagint appears to have had the benefit of these reading instructions in many places.

One example of the significance of the difference between the written text and the marginal instruction for vocalization is to be found in connection with "Though he slay me, yet will I trust in him" (Job 13:15, KJ). This line, thus translated in the King James Version, is often cited to indicate Job's great faith. The problem is that the word vocalized as *lo* has two spellings, and each spelling means something quite different. Spelled one way, it means *not*, spelled another way, it means *in him*. The text itself is spelled to mean *not*, but the marginal instruction shows the word spelled to mean *in him*. The translator of the King James took the marginal instruction as the guide for translation, reading *lo* to mean *in him*, and rendered it "yet will I trust in him." The matter was noted in the Mishnah, and, very likely, the marginal instruction was based on the Mishnah. The latter says that R. Joshua ben Hyrcanus commented on the word *lo* (spelled as *not*) as in the book of Job itself as follows: "Job served God out of love because . . . ." At this point in the Mishnah the line from Job is quoted with *lo* spelled as *in him* (Mishnah, Nashim: Sotah 5:5). The translators of the Revised Standard Version have gone back to read the word vocalized as *lo* to the meaning of the text's *not*, defying the marginal instruction, and have rendered it, "Behold, he will slay me; I have no hope."

There have been many problems associated with the copying of manuscripts. "When each scribe was rapidly multiplying codices, one or even several correct texts were but a drop in the ocean. Each manuscript was not only heir to the errors of its ancestors, but was erring against accuracy on its own account as well."[22] After vowels were introduced, the scribes were allowed considerable license with them, since they were not subject to the same Masoretic regulation as was the consonantal text.

Even with respect to reading aloud and translating, the Mishnah demonstrates some skittishness:

> The story of Reuben [Genesis 35:22] may be read but not translated. The story of Tamar [Genesis 38] may be read and translated. The first story of the calf [Exodus 32:1–20] may be read and translated. The second [Exodus 32:21–25] may be read but not translated. The blessing of the priests (Numbers 6:24–27), the story of David [II Samuel 11:2–17] and Amnon [II Samuel 13:1–4] are not to be read and not to be translated. The chariot [Ezekiel I and X] may not be read as a Haftorah [public reading], although Rabbi Judah allows it. Rabbi Eleazar would not have "make known to Jerusalem" [Ezekiel 16] read as a Haftorah (Mishnah, Moed: Megillah 4:9).

It is better that a letter be rooted out of the Torah than that the divine name shall be publicly profaned (BT, Nashim: Yebamoth 79a), say some of the rabbis of the Talmud.

Tradition has long recognized that the Bible contains emendations by the scribes, the *tikkunei soferim,* modifying the text where it might be offensive to or lacking in respect for God. Thus, for example, the Midrash Rabba indicates that the scribes changed "He that touches you touches the apple of *My* eye" to "He that touches you touches the apple of *His* eye," of Zachariah 2:12 (Midrash: Exodus Rabba 13:1), which is the way it is in the currently available manuscripts.

Over the approximate millennium of its development and the two millennia of its subsequent existence, the text has been subject to innumerable changes, copyings, revisions, reorganizations, and conflations. Various forces have been involved in both the changes and the preservations—simple error, intrinsic indeterminateness of a consonantal text and the intrinsic variation associated with the accompanying oral tradition, the historical mission to preserve the text precisely, and the pressure to bring the text into line with prevailing attitudes and beliefs. Between these forces the text tended both to remain stable as well as to leave a trail of detectable changes that constitute a literary history.

The first printed edition of the Hebrew Bible was published in 1488 in Soncino, a small town in the duchy of Milan. It was followed by an edition printed by Daniel Bomberg in Venice in 1524–1525, edited by Jacob ben Chayyim, which became standard. Kittel's *Biblia Hebraica* is based on the Leningrad manuscript. And, in 1914–1918 von Gall published an edition based on eighty manuscripts of the Samaritan text from the fourteenth and fifteenth centuries.

The Targums are free translations in Aramaic that developed in response to the decline of Hebrew as a spoken language. Both the Babylonian Targum, Onkelos, and the Palestinian Targum, Pseudo-Jonathan, were used extensively by Rashi, and have been central documents in rabbinic scholarship since at least the fifth century A.D.

The Greek translation of the Hebrew Bible, referred to as the Septuagint, and commonly abbreviated as LXX, is the version that had the greatest impact in the history of the Judeo-Christian tradition. It was prepared around the third century B.C. in Alexandria, where there was a large Greek-speaking Jewish population. One account, the *Letter of Aristeas* from around the second century B.C. indicates that 72 Jewish scholars (six from each of the twelve tribes) were summoned by King Ptolemy for the purpose, an account repeated in the Talmud (BT, Moed: Megillah 9a). It was the Bible that Philo read and on which he wrote his extensive commentary. Fragments of Deuteronomy from the Septuagint from about 150 B.C.—from a roll torn up and used in the preparation of a mummy—are in the Rylands Library in Manchester, England. The oldest extant manuscripts of the Septuagint are the Codex Vaticanus and the Codex Sinaiticus, both from the fourth century A.D., and the Codex Alexandrinus from the fifth century.

The principal vehicle of the Bible's impact on Western civilization was this Greek translation, which came into existence some time before the birth of Jesus. There are numerous differences between Hebrew manuscripts and Septuagint manuscripts; however, some of the older Hebrew manuscripts differ from later Hebrew manuscripts but are closer to the Septuagint manuscripts. In its Greek form the Septuagint was the backdrop and reference for the New Testament. It was the major text associated with the spread of the teachings of Judaism to the larger Hellenistic world, and it was critical for the spread of Christian thought. It became the official Bible of the Christian Church.

Discrepancies between the earlier versions of the Septuagint and Hebrew texts promoted several revisions. Aquila, believed to be the same as Onkelos, author of the Targum, made a translation into Greek about 140 A.D. under the supervision of Rabbi Akiva. Other revisions were made by Theodotion and by Symmachus later in the second century A.D. Origen reedited the Greek version in the third century A.D., creating a "Hexapla," a six-columned set of translations and Hebrew text, including Aquila, Symmachus, Theodotion, the old Septuagint, and his own version of the Septuagint.

Latin translations existed in the late second century A.D. St. Jerome prepared the Vulgate, a Latin translation, in the early fifth century, and by the eighth century the Vulgate had become the chief version for the Catholic Church. However, as time went on, elements from older Latin translations became combined with Jerome's. A revision in 1592 under Pope Clement VIII was made official, and it has remained.

The leading commentator on the Old Testament is Rashi, who was born in France in 1040 and died in 1105. He founded a school in 1070, which became a major center of Biblical study in the Jewish world. He has been referred to as the prince of commentators. Most of Rashi's comments, based on rabbinic sources, constitutes a filtering and synthesis of the commentaries that were classic at the time of his writing. His commentary on the Pentateuch was printed in 1475, the first printed Hebrew work. His interpretations have been employed in every subsequent translation of the Hebrew text.

NOTES

1. "But their minds were hardened; for to this day, when they read the old covenant . . ." (II Corinthians 3:14).
2. See Otto Eissfeldt, *The Old Testament: An Introduction,* tr. Peter R. Ackroyd (New York: Harper & Row, 1966), pp. 559 ff.
3. See Eissfeldt, Part one, pp. 9–127.
4. *Confessions of St. Augustine,* tr. Edward B. Pusey (New York: Washington Square Press, 1951), p. 65.
5. Harry M. Orlinsky, *Understanding the Bible through History and Archeology* (New York: KTAV Publishing House, 1972), p. 52.
6. Orlinsky, p. 22.
7. Cecil Roth, "Archaelogy." In *Encyclopaedia Judaica, Vol. 3 (Jerusalem: Keter Publishing House, 1972), p. 305.*
8. Eissfeldt, p. 159.
9. Thomas Hobbes, *Leviathan,* Part III, Ch. 33, 1651.
10. B. Spinoza, *Tractatus theologico-politicus,* Chs. 7 and 8, 1670.
11. "And Moses wrote this Torah and gave it to the priests" (Deuteronomy 31:9).
12. Translation from I. Epstein (ed.), *The Babylonian Talmud. Seder Nezikin.* Vol. II (London: Soncino Press. 1935, pp. 71–72).
13. Eissfeldt, pp. 233 ff.
14. Rudolph Smend, Jr., *Die Erzählung des Hexateuch auf ihre Quellen untersucht* [*The narrative of the Hexateuch examined with reference to its sources*] (1912). Eissfeldt, who accepts Smend's contribution, has redesignated Smend's J_1 by L, to suggest a lay nonpriestly source, and used J without a subscript for Smend's J_2. See Eissfeldt, p. 169.
15. Cuthbert Aikman Simpson, *The Early Traditions of Israel* (Oxford: Basil Blackwell, 1948).
16. Robert Henry Pfeiffer, "A non-Israelite source of the Book of Genesis," *Zeitschrift für Alttestamentliche Wissenschaft,* 1930, *48,* 66–73. A complete enumeration by Pfeiffer of the material in the Hexateuch by presumptive documents, including S, is found in Madelaine S. Miller and J. Lane Miller, *Harper's Bible Dictionary* (New York: Harper & Row, 1961), pp. 700–702. The *Encyclopaedia Judaica* provides detailed information on presumptive documentary sources in the articles on the Pentateuch.
17. Rudolph Kittel et al. (eds.), *Biblia Hebraica,* 7th ed. (Stuttgart: Württembergishe Bibelanstalt, 1951).
18. William Foxwell Albright, *Yahweh and the Gods of Canaan* (London: Athlone Press, 1968), p. 209.

19. See Robert Gordis, *The Biblical Text in the Making: A Study of Kethib-Qere* (New York: KTAV Publishing House, 1971), pp. xxii–xxiii; and Saul Lieberman, *Hellenism in Jewish Palestine* (New York: The Jewish Theological Seminary, 1962), pp. 38–43.

20. Lieberman, pp. 43–46.

21. Deuteronomy 28:30, Jeremiah 3:2; Isaiah 13:16; Zachariah 14:2.

22. Gordis, p. 44.

CHAPTER 6

On Interpretation

MODERN INTERPRETATION

The aim of interpretation is to remain rooted while not being bound. It is commonly—and quite properly—assumed that the Bible contains depths of meaning that are not immediately and directly evident. Even fundamentalists, who take the literal text as infallible, do not refrain from making commentary.

The Bible is no ordinary collection of books. As a literary document, the text has unusual power to stimulate creativity. Discovery, in the etymological sense of the removal of a cover, is a commonplace experience in reading the text. So is recognition. Meanings discovered in the Bible preexist in some sense in every one, as though they had been there before the reading. Perhaps the meanings are universal, residing in the condition of human existence, or in what Jung called the "collective unconscious." Perhaps the preexistence of the meanings in us is the result of our being in a culture in which the text has had a major formative influence. In any case, we live among these meanings.

Scepticism toward the text is itself an essential feature of the history of the Bible in our civilization. There never was a time when some scepticism did not exist, or in which there were no scoffers. At the very least the reported miracles seem to violate the nonmiraculous experience of everyday life.

The scepticism that the text generates is itself a factor in the Bible's power over readers. Scepticism serves to put all testimony into a category with dreams, fantasies, myths, and legends. Ideas and information in this category are taken as less than serious, as outside of "reality" or the main business of living. However, precisely because the biblical stories seem unreal and inconsequential, one can enter into and "play" with them, as it were, and they thus provide a vitality less available in the grim business of everyday, consequential, survival-oriented life. The authors of the Bible have led us into fuller psychological participation in the text by their very challenge to credulity. I hasten to say that I intend this comment in no pejorative sense. It is to their credit rather than their discredit, for the meanings to which they thus lead even the sceptical reader are profound and important.

The idea that the Bible is the word of God and that God sought to communicate with humankind through the Bible is an ancient tradition. To attend to the Bible is to "listen," as in the commandment, "Listen, Israel, YHWH our God, YHWH is one" (Deuteronomy 6:4); and "listen diligently to my commandments . . ." (Deuteronomy 11:13). Two main interpretive questions have been: What did God command? and How may we fulfill the commandments?

Spinoza ushered in the modern approach to the interpretation of the Bible with his *Tractatus Theologico-Politicus* in 1670. Essentially, he converted interpretation to interpretation of the text rather than of God's meanings and God's commandments. He believed that one should approach the Bible with a rational and historical critical attitude, studying its language and contents and attempting to ascertain the relationship between the writing and its historical context. Spinoza argued that Moses did not write the Pentateuch, that it had to be written by someone after Moses's time. Readers should attempt to discover what the author intended, and the relationship between the text and subsequent history.

Work in the modern period has followed the direction sketched out by Spinoza. There is certainly a better understanding of the text than was possible under the traditional assumption of divine authorship, which was often associated with repressive piety, on the one hand, and polemical and apologetic intent, on the other. This point of view impeded the penetration of the text that a more anthropocentric approach allows.

Yet, let us not hold too strictly to the distinction between traditional and modern. That distinction breaks down when we confront Ezekiel's anguished idea that God might deliberately issue defective commandments: "And I also gave them statutes that were no good, and ordinances within which they could not live. And I polluted them in their gifts in that they dedicate all that open the womb, in order that I might destroy them, in order that they would know that I am YHWH" (Ezekiel 20:25–26).

If God might deliberately give defective commandments, or if the biblical text contains a commandment that appears to order children to be killed, then the most "modern" approach to the text is imperative, "modern" being anything that radically changes or modifies practice from tradition. We read this anguished thought in the writing of a priest from the sixth century B.C. It is not so "modern" as to assert that the text was written by humans. It does not challenge the existence of God nor the authenticity of the documents in which the commandments were written. It does not indicate that one should not follow God's commandments.

The passage adds a sardonic element to the character of God that reduces the binding quality of the commandments and makes interpretation essential, at least to find out which are the "statutes that were no good." Ezekiel is alluding to the commandment "Set apart (sanctify) to me every first born, the opener of every womb among the children of Israel, of man and of beast. It is mine" (Exodus 13:2), interpreted literally as a commandment to sacrifice. He does not suggest, as the classical interpretation did, that the commandment does *not* mean literal sacrifice. Rather, he accepts it literally but declares it not a good commandment. It comes from a sardonic trait in God. Should such an intended bad commandment be obeyed? he almost asks openly.

A parent is older and more mature than his young child, yet we are older and more mature than our ancestors in the time of history.

We have the experience of all the years of history between their lives and ours. Not least, we know the possibility of nuclear war, not even imaginable to the author of the story of Noah and the flood. We have access to great bodies of literature that did not even exist at that time. We know how crowded the planet may get to be. We know about totalitarianism that would have been unimaginable to, and the envy of, every tyrant known to the writers of the Bible.

We cannot afford to live with illusions, even those of the Bible. The promotion of illusion for infantilized masses is already too great a part of the history of Western civilization. No longer can people be asked to have faith that a duty demanded of them is both wise and virtuous. People have been told that they should do their duty and that thereby they would find out what they were, as Goethe once expressed it. Today it is more realistic to enjoin people to find out first what they are; from that they may perhaps know what their duty is.

Yet, this is in no way to condemn religion. For religion remains the region of ultimate concern, as Paul Tillich put it. Our being inheres in the regions of our thought, affection, and volition, and those regions are vacuous unless we acknowledge the region of the unmanifest beyond them. I venture the thought—sacrilegious though it might appear—that our ancestors who had a hand in the composition and editing of the text were profoundly involved in work that entailed the sin of idolatry, worshipping a God of their own creation; and that many who live within the context of their work may worship a God fashioned by human beings. For today we are aware, as the work of so many students of the Bible has indicated, that the shaping of the image of God in the text was a human enterprise. If we are to regain an authentic religiosity, it is essential that we refrain from making images of God. The nature of God must remain a mystery. Should we, at any time, come to feel that we have solved the mystery of the characteristics of God, then, indeed, would we be in sin. Should we ever come to believe that we have solved that mystery, all the refreshment of existence associated with human religiosity will be gone.

There is an old Chassidic story which is worth retelling at this

point. A rabbi was fond of repeating that there was nothing completely evil in this world. One of his followers thought that he had
found the ultimate counterexample to this assertion. "Rabbi," he
said, "is it not true that a man who does not believe in God is
completely evil?" The Rabbi answered, "No, not even not believing
in God is completely evil. Suppose someone comes to ask for help.
A believer can dismiss him by saying, 'Go, God will help you.' But
the nonbeliever will have to provide the help himself."

Life devoid of devotion to something external to the self is the
same as death. Without such an object of devotion, one is confronted by origins that have no other end than death itself, wealth that
ends in a pocketless shroud, and power that, while spending itself
only on trivia, can only be its own terminal enjoyment.

However, whatever the illusions the text conjures up, it needs no
protection against disillusionment. Some of what I say in this book
may be taken by some readers as disillusioning. That word, of
course, has two meanings. Denotatively it means to be freed from
illusion and, hopefully, to apprehend what is perhaps more valid and
real. Connotatively, however, the word suggests despair rather than
hope. But the connotation holds only when there is no hope behind
the illusion. I believe that, when the illusion is removed, that which
lies revealed is even more hopeful than the illusion. Over the last
centuries, the work of Copernicus, Darwin, and Freud was all disillusioning, in the denotative sense. But the realities they indicated
allowed greater hopes than those illusions they scattered. Greater
hope in increased understanding is the main focus of all our intellectual work.

I make the imaginative leap into the mind that composed the
words from Ezekiel quoted above. I feel his terror. I imagine the
sense of insight and relief he must have experienced. He saw through
the illusion of the biblical God giving only good commandments,
and possibility was opened for him to reevaluate the messages handed down to him.

I suspect that the earlier biblical scholars of the modern period
who penetrated the text to see its human origins equally experienced
terror and insight and relief. They removed the illusion of the

writing only as the word of God. But through this disillusionment
a better appreciation of the text is possible than ever before in its
long history.

The ultimate aim of studying any text is to understand life the
better. An increased understanding of the text itself is an important
means to this end, but it is only a means. Modern criticism has
devoted itself largely to an increased understanding *of the text.* The
strategy of modern criticism was to place the reader in the time and
the place of the writing as much as possible, and to help the reader
overcome the inevitable bias from reading the text at a different time
and place. Yet, as has been pointed out,[1] there can be a danger in
this approach. One may be so caught in understanding the text from
the viewpoint of the time and place of its composition that it can
no longer be appreciated from a contemporary viewpoint. The appropriate balance comes when the original context enhances contemporary appreciation.

POLITICAL CONTEXT

Political functions are significant for appreciating the biblical
text. The diverse people in that ancient land needed a basis for unity.
The earliest of the major documents that make up the text come to
us from about the time that David and Solomon were consolidating
the kingdom. The promulgators of the text understood the value
that a saga has for promoting unity among diverse peoples. A saga
can raise the sense of worth of a people, and that sense of worth
returns to promote belief in the saga. A saga provides a basis for
union among diverse peoples, a common history and destiny and a
common set of values, perceptions, hopes, and expectations.

The biblical saga that developed provided a vision of a single and
ultimate authority, a god, who was the "God of Gods" (Joshua
22:22) and "Lord of Hosts" (II Samuel 6:2). It provided an image
of God, who was himself free from particular locality but who could
give title to land.

Promoting the notion of common descent for diverse peoples, the saga allowed the construction of political, religious, economic, and military alliances all based upon presumptive kinship ties. Although the saga of the text manifestly deviated from the then-classical conception of divine descent, it managed, as we will see, to keep the myth of divine descent at least latent. While granting powers to kings, it simultaneously incorporated controls over kings by providing a code of law for them to follow, a class of powerful hereditary priests, and authority to prophets. In a nation whose long history was characterized by varieties of subordination to other nations and expulsion, the saga provided a constitution that could unify the people both in the land and in dispersion.

Let us consider some examples that indicate the political character of the text. Chapter 14 of Genesis, within the Abraham narrative, recounts the story of a great war. In this war Lot, the nephew of Abraham, is taken captive. On hearing of the capture, Abraham is said to lead an army from his household of 318 men to rescue Lot. The peace is solemnized by a ritual with Melchizedek, said to be King of Salem and a priest of El Elyon, God Most High.

This chapter is radically different from most of the patriarchal narrative. It speaks of alliances, war, peace treaties, and tithes. It presents a figure of Abraham as warrior that is quite out of character. It is filled with historical and geographical material.

The chapter is explained by Gerhard von Rad as a kind of propaganda story to serve the Davidic dynasty. He suggests that

> . . . it attempts to connect Abraham with the location of the Davidic throne . . . ; for Melchizedek, according to the sacred courtly view, was the type, i.e., the prototype and precursor of the Davidic dynasty. . . . In the insistence of our narrative that Abraham gave him a tithe we see Abraham bowing before the one who is holding the place for the future anointed one. We know about the rift between Jerusalem . . . and the patriarchally faithful country population with whom Yahweh's anointed in Jerusalem did not ingratiate himself, and who were, moreover, very reserved because of the material burdens and taxes that originated with him. . . . It is probable, therefore, that the narrative is directed to observant circles of the liberty-minded population in Judah. . . . Chapter 14 is against this attitude. Abraham, although he did not compromise himself

with any stranger about anything, still bowed to Melchizedek and gave him a tithe.[2]

The story of David and Bathsheba may also be considered from a political point of view. The story bears on the legitimacy of Solomon and his claim to the throne. David sees Bathsheba, the wife of Uriah, one of his soldiers, taking a bath, "and the woman was very good looking" (II Samuel 11:2). David "sent messengers and took her and she came in to him, and he lay with her . . . and she returned to her house. And the woman conceived, and she sent and told to David saying, 'I am pregnant' " (11:5). David tries to persuade Uriah to go home to Bathsheba, hoping that Uriah would then have intercourse with her. Uriah refuses. David then arranges to have Uriah killed by sending him to be abandoned in the thickest part of a battle. After Uriah's death, "David sent and took her to his house and she became a wife to him, and bore him a son" (11:27).

The narrative then indicates that the child dies, and continues. On learning of the death of the child after engaging in mourning activity while the child is but sick, David "rose from the ground," and "washed, and anointed himself, and changed his clothes" (12:20). He then "comforted Bathsheba his wife, and went into her, and lay with her and she bore a son and called his name Solomon" (12:24).

A recent analysis indicates that this story was written during the early years of Solomon's reign, just after he had taken the throne.[3] We know that Solomon's claim to the throne was challenged. We can presume that it was suggested that Solomon was not the son of David but the son of Uriah. The story then serves to establish that Solomon is the legitimate son of David. It certainly does not do credit to David, but it does serve to indicate that Solomon was conceived after any child of Bathsheba who could have been Uriah's. Whatever truth the narrative may have, the story was useful in connection with Solomon's claim to the throne.

The account of the events associated with Moses's having married a Cushite woman may also be cited to exemplify the political character of the text. "And Miriam and Aaron spoke against Moses because of the Cushite woman he had taken" (Numbers 12:1). They challenge him, suggesting that he is no more privileged to engage in intermarriage than anyone else: "Has indeed YHWH spoken only with Moses? Has not YHWH also spoken with and listened to us?" (12:2). At that point YHWH appears in a pillar of cloud, scolds them severely, and makes Miriam leprous as a punishment.

The story clearly suggests an exemption from the injunction against intermarriage for the chief leader. This story also arises around the time of Solomon and would appear to justify Solomon's various marriages to establish cordial relationships with other groups. The characters may be Moses, Miriam, and Aaron, and the setting the wilderness, but the theme alludes to Solomon and his critics.

MANIFEST AND LATENT CONTENT

In Freud's approach to the interpretation of dreams[4] a critical distinction is that between the dream content, the manifest, and the dream thoughts, the latent. The process of fashioning the dream content out of the dream thoughts Freud calls the dream-work. A process of censorship characteristically involved in the dream-work works to exclude from consciousness whatever tendencies would displease it. The censorship process distorts the latent content that presses into consciousness so as to make it consciously unrecognizable.

There are similarities between dream interpretation and biblical exegesis. I have earlier expressed the view that Freud, in his approach to dream interpretation, drew upon the methods of biblical exegesis, especially those more closely associated with mystical strands within Judaism.[5] At one point Freud explicitly identifies his analysis of dreams with interpretation of scripture:

> Examples could be found in every analysis to show that precisely the most trivial elements of a dream are indispensable to its interpretation and that the work in hand is held up if attention is not paid to these elements until too late. We have attached no less importance in interpreting dreams to every shade of the form of words in which they were laid before us. And even when it happened that the text of the dream as we

had it was meaningless or inadequate—as though the effort to give a
correct account of it had been unsuccessful—we have taken this defect
into account as well. In short, we have treated as Holy Writ what previous
writers have regarded as an arbitrary improvisation, hurriedly patched
together in the embarrassment of the moment.[6]

There is an even more profound connection between biblical
exegesis and dream interpretation. Saul Lieberman, the distinguished Talmudic scholar, has cited evidence from the ancient world
to show how methods developed originally for the purpose of analy-
sing dreams were adopted for use in interpreting the Bible.[7] The
chain is then dream interpretation–biblical exegesis–dream interpretation. In this sense the Bible may be regarded as one of the major
dreams of mankind in Western civilization, and thus it calls for
ongoing analysis.

The conviction that human expression is often at best a stammer
is fundamental to the enterprise that Freud began. To extract meaning is often a kindness to, and a healing for, the stammerer. By being
understood, the stammerer is freed from the bondage of unex-
pressed or barely expressed thoughts, feelings, wishes, and buried
memories. To extract meaning out of the expressions of a culture
is to serve it in a similar way. To interpret and find the hidden
meanings is to give life to the authors of the Bible. That we are
ourselves part of the culture informed by them makes the enterprise
a kindness to ourselves as well.

Interpretation always remains incorrigibly speculative. If the
manifest text were exhaustively explicit, there would be no reason
to interpret. But since the manifest text is not exhaustively explicit,
its meanings must always be, to some degree, guess-work. There are
two criteria by which to evaluate speculation. The first criterion is
the degree to which the interpretation provides a coherent, cogent,
and comprehensive vision of the available data. In this case the
available texts constitute the data base. The second criterion is the
relative coherence, cogency, and comprehensiveness of an interpretation compared to other interpretations of the same data. The
application of the second criterion depends on the availability of

alternative interpretations. Thus interpretation is always open to reevaluation when new data arise and new speculations are forthcoming. Furthermore, the addition of any new speculation adds to the basis for evaluating any extant interpretation.

But a license for speculation can also be an invitation for wild or self-serving interpretations. Psychoanalytic and biblical history have had their share of both. One author, in discussing the history of the Bible, aptly says, "Scripture was a wax nose that could be twisted into any desired shape. The desired shape, it turned out, was all too often something outside the Bible itself, an authoritative code of conduct or system of dogma."[8] There are, admittedly, dangers associated with interpretation. Yet, to invalidate interpretation because of the possibility of misuse is hardly an appropriate solution. The fact is that we understand nothing without the aid of imagination; we also understand little if imagination is completely dominant. The tests of coherence, cogency, and comprehensiveness must be made.

I find it useful to attend primarily to theme and secondarily to character and setting in trying to understand biblical narratives. If a biblical narrative answers the questions what (theme), who (character), and when and where (setting), the what would be most important. Indeed, the authors appear to allow themselves considerable looseness with respect to the who, when, and where. I assume that the biblical authors often intended to present the reader with parables, narratives in which only the theme is important, and the particular characters and settings are not crucial. If we follow Freud in his *Interpretation of Dreams*, there is a similar looseness with respect to character and setting in dream-work. Modifying character and setting serves the function of concealment in both dream and parable. Only theme characteristically contains the essential content. One may comfortably dream of some alternative person in an alternative setting, while the dream may be referring to an important theme in one's own life.

If we take the critical feature of the narrative to be theme, we can then recognize a special technique that is characteristic of the biblical writers: to divide a theme among different characters and settings. Thus, as we shall see, the author of the story of the visit of the angel to Mary and Elizabeth in Luke divided the theme of the visit of the angels to Abraham and Sarah in Genesis 18 between the story of Elizabeth and Zacharias and the story of Mary and Joseph.

CLASSICAL INTERPRETATION

It is of value to consider at least briefly the classical approaches to biblical interpretation. Most fundamental are the rules of Hillel. Hillel is a major personality of the Talmud, which cites the great debates between the House of Hillel and the House of Shammai. One of Hillel's major contributors was the development of exegesis as a self-conscious discipline. Hillel's seven hermeneutical principles, likely not original with him but attributed to him, are as follows:

1. One may draw from the lesser to the greater. That which applies in a less important case would certainly apply in a more important case.
2. One may draw inferences from one verse to another on the basis of similarity of words or phrases.
3. A law in one verse applies to all.
4. A law in two verses applies to all.
5. When a generalization is followed by a specification, it restricts the generalization; and when a specification is followed by a generalization, the specification may be extended.
6. A difficulty in a passage may be solved by an analogous passage elsewhere.
7. One interprets words and passages on the basis of context (BT, Avot deRabbi Nathan[9]32a).

Rules 1–6 assume that the mentality associated with the composition of the text is everywhere the same. The traditional understanding, of course, is that the commonality arises from the singularity of God, whose spirit informed every part of the text. The assumption of such a common mentality provides the interpretative license to let one part of the text bear upon one another.

Let us grant that the assumption of a common mentality has considerable validity, even though we may have to hold the theological explanation in abeyance. Today we are very aware that the text is the gathering of various compositions, worked over by many hands; and that one of the aims of the various editors was to make a reasonably unified whole out of it. In this way a common mentality may lie behind the text, even if it does so after the fact.

There is yet another sense in which a common mentality lies behind the text. The content in the text was extremely well known in the culture of the ancient world for a very long time. It was taught; it was memorized. One of the results was that allusion could be used by authors and editors with confidence that it would not be lost on readers or listeners. Allusion can be freely used in a culture where most people have been exposed to a common literary or social heritage. Modern authors have little reason to believe that a specific literary allusion will be recognized, but that was not the case in the ancient world. Thus, for example, when an early Christian read in Mark that, when Jesus called out on the cross, "some of them that stood by, when they heard it, said, Behold, he calls Elijah" (15:35), there was little doubt that this laconic statement called up the story of Elijah bringing the dead back to life: "And YHWH heard the voice of Elijah and the soul of the child returned to within him, and he came back to life" (I Kings 17:22).

The Talmud allowed lifting a letter from one word and adding it to another. The example is from the instructions on the modes of sacrifice, where it says that the priest should "take from the blood of the bullock and carry it to the tent of meeting." By the moving of one letter, this may read that the priest should "take blood from the bullock," more consistent with the rabbinical understanding. Hence "One may remove and add and thus interpret" (BT, Moed: Yoma 48a).

In order to substantiate the view that a husband is his wife's heir, a passage dealing with inheritance on the death of a man is brought to bear: "If his father should have no brothers you shall give his inheritance to his kin" (Numbers 27:11). By lifting a prefix and suffix from a word, and making a new word out of it, one can make this into "you shall give the inheritance of his kin to him," thus establishing the widower's right to his wife's property when she dies. It is explicitly stated that it is permissible for letters to be so detached and interpretations given (BT, Nezikin: Baba Bathra 111b).

The order of letters could also be changed, as in an anagram, to produce new words and new meanings. A word could be taken as an abbreviation, with each letter taken as the beginning of a word. The fact that Hebrew letters are also numbers could be used to draw out implications. So, for example, since the numerical value of *Eliezer* is precisely 318, and since the text indicates that Abraham led a company of 318 (Genesis 14:14), Jewish legend has it that only Eliezer was involved in the conflict. Indeed, it is interesting that even Christian legend followed Jewish legend, allowing that 318 is an allusion to Jesus on the grounds that the numerical value of his name was 318.[10] We find interesting plays on words among the interpretations. For example, when God created Adam, "his name was called *esh* [fire], and she was called *esh* [fire]. What did the Holy One, blessed be He, do? He put His name, YH, between their names,"[11] thus creating *ish* and *ishah*, man and woman. By adding the Y to the word for fire, the word becomes man. By adding H to the word for fire, it becomes woman. Therefore, sexual dimorphism resulted from fire by the addition of two letters of God's name.

Some of these exotic methods of interpretation do not necessarily produce cogent interpretations of the *text*. Such methods can produce meanings that in no sense were ever consciously or even unconsciously intended by the authors. On the other hand, insofar as these interpretations entered into the history of thought in connection with the Bible, they constitute an important part of the cultural context of biblical history. They especially indicate the strength of the conviction that the Bible contains depths of meaning that are not immediately manifest.

NOTES

1. See, for example, Walter Wink, *The Bible in Human Transformation: Toward a New Paradigm for Biblical Study* (Philadelphia: Fortress Press, 1973).
2. Gerhard von Rad, *Genesis: A Commentary,* tr. John H. Marks (Philadelphia: Westminster Press, 1959), pp. 175–176.
3. R. N. Whybray, *The Succession Narrative: A Study of II Samuel 9–20, I Kings 1 and 2* (London: SCM Press, 1968).
4. Sigmund Freud, *The Interpretation of Dreams,* tr. James Strachey (New York: Basic Books, 1955).
5. David Bakan, *Sigmund Freud and the Jewish Mystical Tradition* (Boston: Beacon Press, 1975).
6. Freud, pp. 513–514.
7. Saul Lieberman. *Hellenism in Jewish Palestine,* 2nd ed. (New York: Jewish Theological Seminary, 1962), pp. 47 ff.
8. Delbert R. Hillers, *Covenant: The History of a Biblical Idea* (Baltimore, Md.: Johns Hopkins Press, 1969).
9. This is one of the extracanonical minor tractates, printed following the fourth division, Nezikim, but not part of Nezikim.
10. Louis Ginzberg, *The Legends of the Jews,* Vol. 5 (Philadelphia: Jewish Publication Society, 1955), p. 224.
11 *Pirke De Rabbi Eliezer,* tr. Gerald Friedlander (New York: Benjamin Blom, 1971), p. 88. This was a widely circulated narrative commentary from about the eighth century. It was first printed in 1514 in Constantinople.

CHAPTER 7

Traces of Matrocentrism

Let us now consider the text. Unquestionably, the general impact of the text is to promote patrocentrism, and the associated patrilineality and patriarchy. This feature of the text has come to special prominence with the growth of the women's liberation movement. For example, in *Sexual Politics* Kate Millett asserts that the Bible indicates that God is on the "side of" patriarchy.[1] Mary Daly sees the attitudes concerning the relationship between men and women expressed in the Bible as "malignant."[2]

However, there are strong traces of a prior matrocentrism, with matrilineality and perhaps even matriarchy, in the text. While later writers may have "written over" earlier texts, the traces exist. Since they exist, we might also allow that strong forces prevailed to keep the traces in the text. I will deal with some of these traces in this chapter.

To begin with, in spite of the seemingly main patrilineal thrust of the text, matrilineality remained the essential criterion for the determination of identity among the Jews, the people who sought most explicitly and strenuously to use the text as a detailed guide to conduct in Western civilization. Matrilineality remains, to the present day, the basis for identity as a Jew in rabbinic law. Thus in the Talmud we have: "R. Johanan said on the authority of R. Simeon b. Yohai, . . . Your son by an Israelite woman is called your son, but your son by a heathen is not called your son. Rabina said:

This proves that your daughter's son by a heathen is called your son" (BT, Nashim: Kiddushin 68b; also Nashim: Yevamoth 23a).

Even among the genealogical accounts in the text, which are characteristically patrilineal, we can find allowance of a female link within a male chain as follows: "And Sheshan had no sons but only daughters. And Sheshan had an Egyptian servant and his name was Yarcha. Sheshan gave his daughter to Yarcha his servant as a wife; and she bore him Attai." The genealogical record continues laconically, in the usual fashion, with "And Attai begat Nathan, and Nathan begat . . ." (I Chronicles 2:34–36).

INCEST

The authors' understanding of lineage is revealed in their treatment of incest. It may be assumed that, where the authors appear to see no incest barrier, they did not believe that close kinship prevailed. There are clear indications that some of the authors did not perceive patrilineal kinship to be an incest barrier.

Abraham, fearful for his life, tells Abimelech, the king, that Sarah is his sister (Genesis 20:2). Sarah marries Abimelech. When Abimelech learns that Sarah is Abraham's wife, he confronts Abraham. Abraham replies "And furthermore, it is true that she is my sister. She is the daughter of my father but not the daughter of my mother. And so she became a wife to me" (Genesis 20:12).

If a brother and a sister by a common father, but not a common mother, may marry, then, in the mind of the author (presumably E),[3] lineage that bears on an incest taboo is only matrilineal. Either the author would have us believe that Abraham is telling a gross lie—but there is nothing to suggest that—or the author finds nothing wrong in marrying a sister by a common father but different mother. Sarah is not the daughter of Abraham's mother, and so it is quite all right for him to have married her.

It is certainly the case that the Bible otherwise forbids marriage with a patrilineal sister. In Leviticus it says explicitly, "The nakedness of your sister, the daughter of your father . . . you shall not uncover" (Leviticus 18:9, see also Leviticus 20:17 and Deuteronomy

27:22). But this comes from a later source, the Holiness Code, (Leviticus 17–26), which was incorporated in the fifth century B.C. in the P document. Either the inconsistency of the E contribution to the Abraham narrative escaped the redactors, or their sense of the holiness of the text prevented them from changing it. There has been some suggestion to explain the combined status of wife and sister in the biblical narrative (see Genesis 12:10–20; 26:6–16) on the basis of findings of tablets excavated from the ancient city of Nuzi, in modern Iraq, which date from the 14th century B.C. There it is found that a wife has a higher status if, in addition to marriage, she is also adopted as a sister. However, this is of little help in the Abraham narrative, where such an adoption seems to be precluded by "she is the daughter of my father" (Genesis 20:12).

A similarly indicative story is to be found in II Samuel, arising during the David-Solomon period, early in the history of the text. It also clearly indicates that having a common father is not, in the mind of the author, a barrier to brother-sister marriage. Amnon rapes his paternal sister, Tamar, in the story. David is father to both, but they evidently have different mothers. What is most revealing are the words of protest that the author ascribes to Tamar when Amnon reveals his intentions:

> No, my brother, don't force me. Because no one does such a thing in Israel. Don't do this unclean thing. And as for me, where can I take my shame? And you will become one of the unclean ones in Israel. And now, please speak to the King, because he will not withhold me from you. (II Samuel 13:12–13)

Her objection to having sexual relations with Amnon is that they are not married, not because of incest! On the contrary, Amnon could apparently have his way with her quite legitimately simply by appealing to the king. The social integration of the role of the male in conception had not yet reached the point where it caused an incest barrier.

In Ezekiel's time, around the exile of 597 B.C., the practice of incest between patrilineal siblings must still have existed for him to have protested: "and each man defiles his sister, his father's daughter" (Ezekiel 22:11).

The story of Lot having sexual relations with his daughters is also indicative. That strange story becomes more fully comprehensible if we allow that the social context of the author is matrilineality.

> And Lot went up from Zoar, and lived in the mountain. And his two daughters were with him, because he was afraid to live in Zoar. And he lived in a cave, he and his two daughters. And the first-born said to the younger, "Our father is an old man. And there is no man in the land to come on us in the manner of the whole world. Come we will make our father drunk with wine, and we will lie with him, and we will enliven seed from our father." And they made their father drunk with wine that night. And the first-born went and laid[4] her father; and he did not know when she lay down and when she arose. And the next day came, and the first-born said to the younger: "So, I laid my father yesterday. Let us make him drunk with wine tonight also, and you go in and lie with him, and enliven seed from our father." And they made their father drunk with wine that night too. And the younger rose, and lay with him. And he did not know of her laying down or getting up. And both the daughters of Lot were pregnant from their father. And the first-born bore a son and called him by the name of Moab. He is the father of Moab to this day. And the younger also bore a son and called him by the name of Ben-Ammi. He is the father of the sons of Ammon to this day. (Genesis 19:30–38)

There is certainly no doubt that the author is fully aware of the male involvement in conception. However, the story strongly suggests that the social integration of this fact is incomplete. For there is no hint in the text that the moral code of the authors is affronted by the action of the women. While it is true that later commentators attempted to apologize for Lot's daughters on the grounds of their own defense—that otherwise they would not have children—the heinousness of incest would have been too great to excuse it in any way. We can only presume that patrilineality had not yet been established sufficiently strongly to make the act of incest with a father strictly taboo. For if the daughter's lineage from the father

is not fully established, then sexual relations with him are not incestuous. In the same way that Abraham could marry his patrilineal
sister, so could Lot legitimately impregnate his dauthers. If lineage
is only through the female, then sexual relations with a wife's daughter is not incestuous.

LINEAGE AND GEOGRAPHICAL DISTRIBUTION

Julian Morgenstern, biblical scholar and president of Hebrew
Union College, advanced the hypothesis that prior to the establishment of the Kingdom under David the people were organized on the
basis of matrilineal clans; these matrilineal clans were subsequently
united into patrilineal tribes which took the names of eponymous
male ancestors; a saga indicating that these male ancestors were the
sons of a single male, Jacob or Israel, was subsequently developed;
and this unification was associated with a shift from matrilineality
to patrilineality.[5]

Jewish myth, which carries very archaic material, endowed each
tribe with a female ancestor, even at the "expense" of allowing
incest. The myth provided each of Jacob's sons except Joseph with
a twin-sister wife. And Joseph was destined to marry his sister's
daughter. Thus we read in *Pirke De Rabbi Eliezer:*

> . . . in seven years there were born unto Jacob eleven sons (or tribes) and
> one daughter. And all of them were born, each with his partner with him,
> except Joseph, whose partner was not born with him, for Asenath, the
> daughter of Dinah, was destined to be his wife, and (also) except Dinah,
> whose partner was not born with her.[6]

In this myth the tribes in each case descend not only from one
of Jacob's male children, but from one of Jacob's female children
as well.

For Joseph, who according to the text had a wife from Egypt, the
Bible conveniently provides a special adoption ceremony to correct
for the defective matrilineality of his sons. The authors ascribe to
Jacob the following words: "And now, your two sons who were born

to you in the land of Egypt before I came to you into Egypt, they are mine. Ephraim and Manasseh will be to me just as Reuben and Simeon" (Genesis 48:5).

It is instructive to compare the kinship patterns as they are given in the text with the approximate geographical distribution of the tribes prior to the establishment of the kingdom, as the biblical text allows it to be reconstructed.

According to the text, Jacob has two wives, Leah and Rachel. Leah has a handmaiden by the name of Zilpah. Rachel has a handmaiden by the name of Bilhah. Leah has six sons, Reuben, Simeon, Levi, Judah, Issachar, and Zebulun. Her handmaiden Zilpah has two sons, Gad and Asher. Rachel has two sons, Joseph and Benjamin; and Joseph has two sons, by an Egyptian wife, Ephraim and Manasseh. Rachel's handmaiden, Bilhah, has two sons, Dan and Naphtali.

If we examine the map showing the reconstructed geographical distribution, we note that there is substantial correspondence of geographical location with the matrilineal eponymous ancestors. The Southern Kingdom is essentially the Kingdom of Leah in the name of her sons Judah, Reuben, and Simeon. The Northern Kingdom is essentially the Kingdom of Rachel, in the name of the sons of her son Joseph, Manasseh and Ephraim, and her son Benjamin. Gad, Asher, part of Dan and Naphtali, the sons of the handmaidens, correspond to more remote areas. The youngest sons of Leah, Zebulun and Issachar to the north, are exceptions in the neat north-south division.

To the east and to the south we have, respectively, the Ammonites, the Moabites, the Edomites, the Ishmaelites, and the Midianites. According to the story, Moab is the offspring of Lot and his first daughter, and Ammon is the offspring of Lot and his second daughter; the Edomites are the offspring of Esau, twin of Jacob, from Rebekah, who is the matrilineal aunt of Rachel and Leah; the Ishmaelites are from Hagar; and the Midianites are the offspring of Keturah, the wife that Abraham took after Sarah's death.

Thus each geographical group is associated with a female progenitor. The text ingeniously unites these peoples in terms of kinship saga with kinship distance reflecting geographical and political reali-

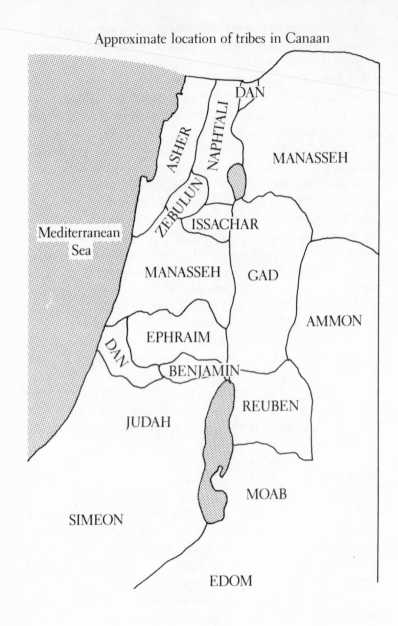

Approximate location of tribes in Canaan

ties. The saga's neatness in integrating kinship with geographical and political realities would give credibility to the belief that the saga was based on realities at the time of writing, rather than being an accurate depiction of the actual history of lineage.

Furthermore, the biblical text even allows the possibility of a female lineage for the wives of the patriarchs corresponding to the Abraham-Isaac-Jacob line. Rebekah, the wife of Isaac, comes from the same household as Sarah, Abraham's sister; and Leah and Rachel, the wives of Jacob, come from the same household as Rebekah. We thus are given a parallel Sarah-Rebekah-Leah-Rachel lineage quite independent of Abraham-Isaac-Jacob as ancestors of the Israelites.

We may then speculate that one of the purposes of the patrilineal kinship saga was to unify peoples, who were originally matrilineally identified, into a larger unit. The device of the saga was to assign female ancestors as wives or concubines of males.

The matrilineal orientation is clearly shown in the Abraham part of the saga alone. Abraham has three spouses, Hagar, Sarah, and Keturah, presumably the separate ancestors of different clan lineages. Not all the offspring of Abraham are Israelites; the Israelites stem only from Sarah. Sarah is more definitively the ancestor of the Israelites than Abraham. Different peoples are associated with Hagar and with Keturah. The idea of a single male ancestor, Abraham, whose name means "father of many nations," could serve to integrate not only the peoples of the kingdom but peoples from the outlying areas, which was one of Solomon's aims. The assigned kinship connections are probably metaphors for actual or desired patterns of political relationships. It should be noted that Solomon's efforts to integrate territory on the basis of marriages was quite analogous to the unificiation-through-marriage theme in the saga.

COVENANTS AND THE MYSTERY OF SHADAY

The biblical idea of covenant is generally associated with males rather than with females. The critical covenantal passages occur in connection with males. Yet the text does provide a passage in which a covenant is made by God with a female, Hagar, the concubine of Abraham and the mother of Ishmael.

An angel of the YHWH appears to Hagar in the wilderness and says: "I will multiply your seed greatly and it will not be countable because of its size" (Genesis 16:10). This promise is precisely parallel to the corresponding address of YHWH to Abraham: " 'Please look to the sky and count the stars, if you be able to count them,' and he said to him: 'Thus will your seed be' " (Genesis 15:5).

Were the parallel complete, we would have a corresponding convenantal passage with Sarah, since Abraham is father to both Ishmael and Isaac. Rather, we have one covenant made with Hagar, on behalf of her son Ishmael and his descendants, and another covenant made with Abraham. The covenant with Abraham is not on behalf of all of Abraham's offspring but only on behalf of Sarah's offspring. Indeed, there is the rather peculiar statement addressed to Abraham about Isaac, "Take your son, your only son" (Genesis 22:2), when, according to the narrative at that point, Abraham has two sons, Ishmael and Isaac. Thus even the covenant with Abraham would appear to be a covenant with Sarah, or at least on behalf of Sarah, corresponding to the covenant with Hagar.

There are two mysteries in the text that may be clarified by considering them together. These are the meanings to be attached to one of the names of God, eL SHaDaY, and Sarah's name, SaRaY, as it first appears in the text before being changed to SaRaH. I suggest that bringing these names to bear on each other might clarify the meaning of both.

SHaDaY has characteristically been translated as Almighty, and SaRaY as princess. The grounds for both translations are not considered to be very strong.

In Exodus we find an effort to put together the name of eL SHaDaY with the name of YHWH: "And Elohim spoke to Moses and said to him: 'I am YHWH. And I appeared to Abraham and to Isaac and to Jacob as eL SHaDaY and my name YHWH I did not make known to them' " (Exodus 6:3).

EL SHaDaY characteristically occurs in Genesis together with a blessing for fertility:

I am eL ShaDaY. Walk before me and become whole. And I will give my covenant between Me and you, and I will multiply you very much. (Genesis 17:1–2)

And eL ShaDaY bless you, and make you fruitful and multiply you. . . . (Genesis 28:3)

And Elohim said to him, I am eL SHaDaY. Be fruitful and multiply. . . . (Genesis 35:11)

And Jacob said to Joseph "EL SHaDaY appeared to me at Luz in the land of Canaan and blessed me. And said to me, 'behold I will make you fruitful and multiply you and I will make you a multitude of people, and I will give this land to your seed after you as a possession forever.' " (Genesis 48:3–4)

It occurs once without the fertility blessing, but in connection with Jacob's fear that he would be bereft of his children (Genesis 43:14).

Interestingly enough, eL SHaDaY otherwise appears in the Pentateuch, without the allusion to fertility, only in the passage of Balaam, the heathen soothsayer called by the King of Moab to curse Israel (Numbers 24:4,16); and in the passage that was, according to the rabbis of the Talmud, the only passage in the Pentateuch written by Moses besides "his own book" (see p. 34).

This suggests a fertility association with the name eL SHaDaY. SHaD means breast and is so used throughout the Bible; for example, Ezekiel 23:21, Hosea 9:14, Ezekiel 23:21, Isaiah 32:12, and other places. Rashi has God saying, "I will bless her with nursing of breasts (SHaDaYiM)" (Genesis 17:16), and Sarah saying, "that these withered breasts (SHaDaYiM) shall yield milk" (Genesis 18:-12) The word is used quite precisely to mean breast.

Let us now consider Sarah's names. In the early part of the text she is Sarai. The change from Sarai to Sarah is in Genesis 17:15: "Do not call her name SaRaY, but SaRaH shall be her name."

One of the most common scribal errors in copying texts was the interchanging of the *resh* (ר) and *daleth* (ד). Because of the great similarity between them in their written form, a *daleth* (ד) could easily be interpreted as a *resh* (ר) and vice versa in a worn text.[7]

Since the consonantal text does not distinguish *shin* (שׁ) from *sin*

(שׁ), eL SHaDaY (eL SaRaY) could have the meaning of either *god breast* or *god Sarai,* or both.

Sarai's name gets changed to Sarah. If we allow the possibility of the interchangeability of *resh* (ר) and *daleth* (ד) in the text, Sarah's name could be SaDaH, which means field. Indeed, Isaiah 32:12 has a play on these words: "On the breasts [SHaDaYiM] they lament for the delightful fields [SDaY]."

Sarah's name as breast and/or field is then parallel to the meaning of Abraham's name. As his name is taken from his relationship to offspring, meaning father, Sarai's name as SHaDaY, breast, would similarly take its meaning from the relationship to offspring. In the modification of her name to SaRaH, or SaDaH, as field, it means the place where the seed, the biblical expression for the male sexual exudate, is deposited. In fact, SaDaY meaning field or land is a rare form of SaDaH, and is so found in Jeremiah 4:17 and elsewhere.[8] The word SaDaH has also been linked to mountain, as has SHaDaY;[9] and a metaphorical connection of mountain to breast strongly suggests itself.

The word SaDaH, meaning field, has, indeed, characteristically been interpreted as woman in the Jewish tradition. In the *Pirke De Rabbi Eliezer,* the author comments on "And it came to pass when they were in the field" (Genesis 4:8), as follows: " 'In the field' means woman, who is compared to a field." In another manuscript of the *Pirke De Rabbi Eliezer* it is indicated that this derives from "But if a man find the damsel that is betrothed in the field" (Deuteronomy 20:19). In still another manuscript of *Pirke De Rabbi Eliezer* this idea is illuminated with "For man is the tree of the field" (Deuteronomy 20:19). "My father begot me, my mother gave me birth. She was the furrow in which his seed was sown' " The notion of woman as field is to be found in various hermetic and alchemical writings and in Euripides,[10] and it corresponds to the contemporary idea of Mother Earth. All of this would be consistent with a change of Sarah's name to SHaDaY and SaDaH instead of SaRaY and SaRaH, as it is in the texts available to us.

It should also be pointed out that the word SHeiD, with the same consonants but vocalized differently, means idol. "They sacrificed to the SHeiDiYM which were not gods" (Deuteronomy 32:17).

"And they sacrificed their sons and their daughters to the SHei-diYM" (Psalms 106:37). The commonest type of religious object uncovered from the variety of excavations in the area of ancient Palestine are figurines of bare-breasted women. They have been found in every major excavation in Palestine. The very quantity of these figurines would indicate their great significance in the culture that gave rise to the text. They have been dated from a thousand years before the establishment of the kingdom to four hundred years after its establishment. Some figures are holding stalks or serpents. In some the hands are holding the breasts, in some one hand is holding a breast while the other is over the genital region. Some of the figures clearly suggest pregnancy. Subsidiary evidence in terms of inscriptions and the like leave little doubt that the figures were used for religious purposes. Patai has indicated that there is considerable evidence to indicate a historical condition in which female divinities were widely accepted.[11]

THE GENDER OF NOAH

Although in fact all human beings must have both a mother and father biologically, the human accounting of lineage may not necessarily take account of that fact. Thus lengthy lineages are characteristically given in the Bible simply in terms of the male who childed a male, and so on.

There is reason to believe that the text that has reached us may have been tampered with so that the Noah figure was changed from a female to a male. However, clues remain that can lead us to what might be called an *undernarrative,* a story which was modified in the telling of another story. Indeed, the whole history of story telling is a history of stories which have been changed to make new stories, of narratives created by changing the elements of their progenitor undernarratives, which may still live within the younger narratives.

Our basic notion that the fact of paternity was unknown at some time in the history of the world, and that the integration of the information about the role of males in conception took a long time, would allow the possibility of some prior condition in which lineage, if it meant anything at all, was reckoned through females. Noah is the major progenitor of all the rest of humankind, everyone else having been destroyed in the flood, according to the text. A mentality that conceived of lineage primarily as through the female would be likely to conceptualize the progenitor of the rest of humankind as female.

Does the text have anything in it to even arouse the suspicion that Noah may be female? The text that we have presents Noah as manifestly male, and only by what may seem extremely devious thinking could it be otherwise. Indeed, it might be argued that Noah had to be male in the mind of the author since the text we have provides a wife for Noah. Yet we must always keep in mind that, in spite of the great efforts that were made for accurate copying, especially in the more recent centuries, there was ample opportunity for textual tampering. But let us consider some of the Noah text.

Noah gets drunk and lies naked in his (her) tent. Ham, the father of Canaan, sees the nakedness of Noah and tells of it to his brothers Shem and Japheth, who take a garment, lay it on their shoulders, and, walking backward, cover their father. When Noah awakens from his wine, he puts a curse on Canaan that he should be a servant or slave (eVeD) to Shem and Japheth (Genesis 9:21–27).

This story contains some peculiarities which might be clues to an undernarrative:

The consonantal text would indicate that Noah was in *her* tent: "And he drank of the wine, and was drunk. And he was uncovered within *her* tent [aHaLaH]" (v. 21), the suffix, H, being feminine and characteristically pointed to read aH. However, the vowel has been added to the text so that it is vocalized as *his* tent. Rashi takes pains to point out: "It is written aHaLaH (her tent)." Rabbinical interpretation has suggested that Noah might have been in his wife's tent, at least accepting this reading as "her tent" (Midrash: Genesis Rabba 36:4).

The observation might be added that, in the text, tents are often associated with women, and this association may itself be read as a hint of matrilineality. We find, for example, "And he [Jacob] went out of Leah's tent, and entered Rachel's tent" (Genesis 31:33). And when Isaac receives his bride, he takes her not into a tent associated with his father but into his mother's tent: "And Isaac brought her into the tent of his mother Sarah" (Genesis 24:67). This trace of matrilineality is maintained to the present day in the Jewish marriage ritual, which takes place under the *chupah,* the marriage canopy.[12]

What is heinous about what Ham did? If a male Noah had undressed himself in his drunken state, in the tent, Ham would not have known of it until he entered the tent. If Noah were male, and Ham, his son, were also male, what violence did Ham do by seeing his father naked? Furthermore, Ham told his brothers about it, and they modestly covered him.

There is ample evidence throughout the text to indicate that the expression "uncover nakedness" is not intended literally but is rather a euphemism for improper sexual activity (see Leviticus 18:6 ff.). What is unusual is that in this instance the euphemism is rendered not by the words "uncover nakedness" but by a narrative of Ham seeing his parent naked. One rabbinical interpretation reads it as a euphemism meaning either sodomy or castration or both (BT, Nezikim: Sanhedrin 70a).

The heinousness becomes evident if we allow Noah, in her tent, as female: Ham took sexual advantage of his mother in her drunken state.

Another peculiarity of this story is that Noah puts a curse on *Canaan.* Noah does not curse the offender, Ham. Why Canaan? Canaan is the son of Ham, possibly his youngest since he is cited last: "And the sons of Ham, Cush, and Mizraim, and Put, and Canaan" (Genesis 10:6). If Noah was Ham's mother, and Ham violated the son-mother incest taboo, then Canaan was the product of this union. In this light it is clearer why Noah should put a curse on Canaan. The rabbinical explanation is that the castrated Noah, deprived of his capacity to have a fourth son, puts a curse on Ham's fourth son (BT, Nezikin: Sanhedrin 70a).

Such criminal and bastard origins of Canaan would have had great political significance at one time. Indeed, if the "female version" of the story existed, its political motivation is patent. The Canaanites are the classical enemy. A story of such unseemly origins of an eponymous Canaan, who even bore a curse from his mother to be a slave or servant to his brothers, would have been very powerful. The upshot is clear: "Cursed be Canaan. A servant of servants shall he be unto his brothers. . . . Blessed be YHWH, the god of Shem, and let Canaan be their servant. God enlarge Japheth . . . and let Canaan be their servant" (9:25–27).

It is of some value to consider the injunction against parent-child incest found in Leviticus. It suggests some textual tampering. The text reads, "The nakedness of your father, and the nakedness of your mother, you shall not uncover. She is your mother. You shall not uncover her nakedness" (18:7). It is to be noted that there is a clear imbalance in the injunctions with respect to father and mother. The first part mentions both father and mother, but the elaboration is with respect to the mother only. I would suggest that "The nakedness of your mother you shall not uncover. She is your mother. You shall not uncover her nakedness" perhaps existed prior to an awkward addition of "the nakedness of your father."

Given that considerably lesser hints in the text have been the subject of elaborations and legends in the history of interpretation, it is easy to ask why this almost obvious hint in connection with Noah has not, at least as far as I can tell, been explored. Even if it was developed and suppressed, there should be at least some trace of the suppression.

I suggest that such a trace is to be found in Rashi, written in such a way that only the most careful reading would reveal it.

Let us examine Rashi's notes to the Noah-Ham story. As I have already indicated, Rashi takes pains to indicate that Noah was in *her* tent, aHaLaH.[13] Rashi states that aHaLaH is an "allusion to the ten tribes who were called by the name of Samaritans who were evil on account of the wine," and he goes on to tell us that Samaria was called aHaLaH.

What might Rashi have intended by such an observation beyond the association to wine? The identification of aHaLaH with Samaria is an allusion to Ezekiel. Let us conjecture that Rashi expects the diligent reader to turn to the place indicated in Ezekiel, where aHaLaH is identified with Samaria: "And their names were aHaLaH the older, and aHaLiYBaH her sister. And they became mine. And they bore sons and daughters. And their names, Samaria is aHaLaH and Jerusalem is aHaLiYBaH" (Ezekiel 23:4).

We note first of aHaLaH that Ezekiel has her engaged in whoredom with her Assyrian near ones (or relatives): "And aHaLaH whored under me, and she doted on her lovers, Assyrian near ones" (Ezekiel 23:5). Rashi possibly is hinting that the Noah story alludes to incest.

Further, aHaLaH, aHaLiYBaH appear to be terms of a series. Is there a third term to the series? One is indicated by the fact that Ezekiel indeed refers to a third sister, Sodom, in addition to Samaria and Jerusalem. Addressing Jerusalem, he says, "And your older sister is Samaria . . . and your younger sister is Sodom . . ." (Ezekiel 16:46). At this point, it appears that we have reached a dead end. For we do not have the name of the third sister, a name for Sodom. The first is aHaLaH and the second, aHaLiYBaH, a sequence formed by adding to the preceding term. We may presume that Rashi expects us to provide the third term from the biblical names, and we guess aHaLiYBaMaH, a name that occurs in Genesis 36 several times. We then have aHaLaH, aHaLiYBaH, aHaLiYBaMaH.

Chapter 36 of Genesis is devoted to the genealogies associated with Esau, beginning with, "And these are the generations of Esau. . . ." In this chapter, as Rashi is very careful to point out, there are several relationships that must be interpreted as indicating bastardry. All of Esau's wives, including aHaLiYBaMaH are "the daughters of Canaan" (36:2). Thus, at the very least, we have a link back to the story of Noah, who placed a curse on Canaan. In Rashi's interpretations Chapter 36 is an inventory of incest: "The scripture tells you that all of them were the children of bastardry" (note to 36:2). A pivotal figure in these incestuous bastardries is aHaLiYBaMaH. She is the daughter of *two* men, her father and her grandfather, her grandfather, Zibeon, having had sexual intercourse with his son's (Anah's) wife, "and aHaLiYBaMaH issued from both of them" (note to 36:2). This same Zibeon, according to Rashi, also had sexual intercourse with his own mother, and thus begat Anah (note to 36:24), the co-father of aHaLiYBaMaH. In addition, aHaLiYBaMaH, the wife of Esau, was impregnated by Eliphaz, Esau's son by Adah, giving rise to the bastard Korach (note to 36.5).

I believe that leading us to this chapter and commenting on it in this manner was Rashi's way of explicating the Noah story, telling us that Canaan, the product of son-mother incest, the ancestor of all these bastards, is himself a bastard. Of course, there is no certainty that this was Rashi's intention rather than only an accidental concatenation. This is as far as I can carry the argument that Rashi concurred in the interpretation of Noah as the mother violated by her son Ham to produce Canaan.

PREROGATIVES OF WOMEN

There is a sharp contrast in the value of children to parents between biblical time and contemporary urban-industrial life. Having children and keeping their continuing loyalty are of great value in the biblical text. Enlargement of the number of children was associated with enlargement of wealth, enlargement of the number of workers for caring for flocks, provision of warriors who could defend against enemies and guarantors of maintenance in old age, and even establishment of ties with kings, as in the story of Joseph's establishing a connection with Pharaoh for the rest of his family.

Given the value of children, the text suggests a struggle between the sexes over prerogative with respect to them. Women's great desire for children is variously indicated in the text. "And Rachel saw that she bore no children to Jacob. And Rachel envied her sister. And she said to Jacob, 'Give me children. If not I am dead' " (Genesis 30:7). When she has a son, she says "Elohim has ended my disgrace" (Genesis 30:23). Leah, who is less loved by Jacob than her sister, hopes to endear herself to her husband: "Elohim has endowed me with a good dowry. Now my husband will honor me because I have born to him six sons" (30:20). The well-known story of Solomon's threat to divide a baby in half in the conflict between the two women over its possession (I Kings 3:16–28) may well reflect the value of children to their parents rather than just maternal love.

Pseudo-matrilineality, in the form of assigning the motherhood of maidservants' children to their mistresses, appears to be a common social reality that also speaks to the "ownership" of children by their mothers. This pseudo-matrilineality may be understood as a step toward a corresponding relationship of fathers to their children. "And Sarai said to Abram 'Here now that YHWH has restrained me from bearing, go in, pray you, into my handmaiden. Maybe I can be builded up from her'" (Genesis 16:2). Rachel says to Jacob: "Here is my maid Bilhah. Go into her and she will bear on my knees. And I too will be builded up from her" (Genesis 30:3).

When Bilhah has a son, Rachel says that Elohim has given *her* a son (Genesis 30:6). When Bilhah has a second son, Rachel rejoices over her envied sister, saying that she has "prevailed" over her sister Leah in her "wrestlings of God" (Genesis 30:8). And when Leah believes that she can no longer bear children, she too gives Jacob her handmaiden and has two sons that way (Genesis 30:9–13).

The relative power of Abraham and Sarah with respect to Ishmael, the son of Sarah's handmaiden, would indicate that, in the minds of the authors, Ishmael is more Sarah's, through her ownership of Hagar, than Abraham's. On two occasions Sarah exerts her prerogative with respect to Ishmael—once when Ishmael is still in Hagar's womb, and once when Ishmael is a youth. After Sarai has asked Abraham to impregnate Hagar on her behalf, she has Abraham drive her out (Genesis 16:5–6). Then again, Sarah orders Abraham: "Cast out this bondswoman and her son. For the son of this bondwoman shall not inherit with my son, with Isaac" (Genesis 21:10). The text hints at both patrilineal prerogative and Sarah's ignobility, that "the thing was very evil in the eyes of Abraham on account of his son" (Genesis 21:11). The text nonetheless has Elohim intercede in defense of Sarah and with a seeming compromise: "And Elohim said to Abraham, 'Let it not be evil in your eyes in connection with the boy and your bondswoman. In all that Sarah says to you, listen to her voice. Because in Isaac seed will be called to you. And also the son of the bondswoman I will make into a people, because he is your seed'" (Genesis 21:12–13). Abraham defers and drives Hagar and Ishmael into the wilderness.

One of the most classically troublesome stories in the text has been that of Jacob getting the birthright from Esau by fraud. At the instigation of his mother, Rebekah, Jacob disguises himself as Esau and receives the blessing from his father Isaac (Genesis 27). The whole legal tradition associated with the text would indicate that anything obtained by fraud is not rightfully possessed by the one who gains by the fraud. Yet Jacob's claim is considered valid.

The difficulty vanishes, however, if we understand the birthright to be the prerogative of the mother. For although Jacob and Esau are both the children of Rebekah, the story is unambiguous that it is Rebekah's wish that Jacob should receive the blessing. Thus, whatever the mechanism of transmission may be, Rebekah's wish prevails. True, the authors of the text defer formally to patrilineal prerogative in having Isaac give the blessing. But the story makes it clear that he acts out her will, acting in her place. The matrilineal prerogative for the transmission of rights to offspring is maintained, however covered by a ceremonial patrilineal transmission.

The siring services of males are indicated as the property of women. Thus Leah purchases Jacob's siring services from Rachel. According to the text, Leah's son Reuben finds mandrakes in the field and gives them to his mother. When Rachel asks Leah for the mandrakes, Leah sells them to her in return for Jacob's siring services. When Jacob comes in from the field in the evening, Leah goes out to meet him and says: "Into me you will come, because in trade I have traded you with my son's mandrakes." Jacob appears to accept the transaction as legitimate: "And he lay with her that night" (Genesis 30:16).

The legitimacy of claims for siring services is indicated in the law of the levirate, which provided that if one brother dies without a son then the "husband's brother shall go on her, and take her to himself as a wife, and do the duty of a husband's brother" (Deuteronomy 25:5).

The text provides a lovely substantiation of the legitimacy of the levirate, and thereby the right of women to siring services, in the story of Judah and Tamar. Er, Judah's son, dies, leaving a widow by the name of Tamar. Judah commands another of his sons, Onan: "Go in to your brother's wife, and perform the duty of a husband's brother to her, and raise seed to your brother" (Genesis 38:8). Onan, however, "wasted it on the ground so as not to give seed to his brother" (Genesis 38:9). Judah returns Tamar to her father's household to wait, with the promise that when another of his sons, Shelah, is grown, she could have him as a husband. However, Tamar notes that Shelah grows up "and that she was not given to him as a wife" (Genesis 38:14). Then Tamar, pretending that she is a prostitute, stands at a place where she knows Judah will pass. He offers her a kid from his flock as payment for allowing him to "come into" her, and he leaves her with his signet, cord, and staff as a pledge: "He gave them to her, and came into her, and she conceived by him" (38:18). When he tries to redeem the pledge, she cannot be found. Presently, Judah learns that Tamar is pregnant, and he orders that she be burnt for her harlotry. She indicates, however, that she is with child by the man whose pledge she holds. Judah then acknowledges the pledge and says: "She was more righteous than I was" (Genesis 38:26).

The selection of wives for sons appears to be sometimes the prerogative of the mother. Hagar selects a wife for her son, Ishmael: "And he [Ishmael] dwelt in the wilderness of Paran; and his mother took a wife for him from the land of Egypt" (Genesis 12:21). Rebekah says to Isaac, in the Revised Standard Version, "I am weary of my life because of the Hittite daughters. If Jacob take a wife from one of the Hittite daughters, such as these, of the daughters of the land, what good will life be to me?" (Genesis 27:46).

Let us examine this last quotation a bit more deeply. This particular verse demonstrates how translation forces choices in interpretation. Consider the "I am weary of my life" in the Revised Standard Version translation. The Hebrew word for life, CHaY, not only means life but is also used to indicate kinsfolk. It appears in I Samuel 18:18 and is there translated in the Revised Standard Version, "Who am I, and who are my *kinsfolk*. . . ?" The word that is characteristically translated as "I am weary," KaZTY, can also mean "I am cut off." The word is found in Deuteronomy 25:12 (V'KaZoTaH) to designate punishment. The Revised Standard Version translates the verb so: "Then you shall cut off her hand. . . ."

If we apply these meanings to Genesis 27:46, Rebekah is saying, "I will be cut off from my kinsfolk. . . ." instead of "I am weary of my life." Thus Rebekah's motive for her son to seek a wife from the house from which she came might well be that she should not be cut off from her matrilineal line. Similarly, "what good will life be to me?" might be otherwise rendered, "why do I have kinsfolk?"— Genesis 27:46 is then: "I will be cut off from my kinsfolk because of the Hittite daughters. If Jacob take a wife from the Hittite daughters such as these, of the daughters of the land, why do I have kinsfolk?"

MATRILOCALITY: REBEKAH

Matrilocality is frequently associated with matrilineality. There are several indications in the text that a matrilocal social context conditioned the biblical narratives.

Immediately succeeding the story in which Eve is created out of Adam's rib, the text enjoins: "Therefore should a man leave his father and his mother and cling to his wife and they will be as one flesh" (Genesis 2:24). The injunction is clearly matrilocal.

The story of Samson indicates that he had a matrilocal marriage. "And it was afterward in the days of the wheat harvest that Samson visited his wife with a kid. And he said, 'I will go to my wife in the room.' And her father would not allow him to go. And her father said, 'Because you hated her, so I gave her to your companion' " (Judges 15:1–2).

Until relatively recent times the custom of *kest* existed among the Jews of Eastern Europe.[14] The groom, typically a young scholar still engaged in Talmudic studies, would enter the household of his bride and live there for several years. The custom has become rare in modern times. However, when it prevailed, it was consistent with the matrilocality indicated in the text.

The story of Rebekah's departure to become the wife of Isaac is particularly revelatory with respect to the tensions associated with matrilocality. According to the text, Abraham, in his old age, sends his servant back to his land of birth and family, equally Sarah's land of birth and family, to get a wife for Isaac (Genesis 24:4). The servant expresses concern that "perhaps the woman will not wish to follow" him (Genesis 24:5). This suggests that for the woman to leave with him might entail a violation of a matrilocal social norm. Abraham extracts an oath that the servant will not take Isaac back to the matrilocal location (vs. 6–9). At the well the servant encounters Rebekah, described as "Rebekah . . . who was born to *Bethuel the son of* Milcah, the wife of Nahor, brother of Abraham" (Genesis 24:15). She draws water for him; and he gives her gifts. He inquires whose daughter she is, asking whether there is room in her father's house to lodge in (v. 23). She replies that she is the "daughter of *Bethuel the son of* Milcah who was born to Nahor" (v. 24), and that there is room to lodge. The servant identifies himself. She runs and tells "her mother's house" about him (v. 28). Rebekah's brother, Laban, runs out to meet him, invites him in, and entertains him and his party. The servant explains his mission, recounting his meeting with Rebekah and how she told him that she was "the daughter of *Bethuel son of* Nahor whom Milcah bore unto him" (v. 47). He begs for an answer. Then Laban and *Bethuel* (Milcah) answer (v. 50) and give their consent (v. 51). The servant gives presents to Rebekah and to "her brother and her mother" (v. 53). The "brother and mother" seek to delay her departure, but the servant protests (vs. 55–56). They ask Rebekah what her wishes are, and she agrees to go. They bless her, addressing her as "our sister" (v. 60). And Rebekah departs with the servant.

In the opinion of some critics all the words I have italicized are by a later hand and did not exist in the basic documents that made up the text. In v. 50 this later hand substituted Bethuel for Milcah.[15] It is also to be noted that later in the text, in 29:10, Laban is said to be the son of Nahor not of Bethuel.

Although the text has the servant asking for lodging in her "father's" house (v. 23), Rebekah runs to her "mother's" house (v. 28). If we go back to the presumptive original, prior to the redactor's hand, the negotiation is with Rebekah's brother and mother and not with her father. The servant gives presents to the "brother and mother" and not to the father.

The text appears to be a rather clumsy effort to change a matrilo-cally oriented story to a patrilocally oriented one. If we accept the hypothesis of these critics, Rebekah would be the daughter of Mil-cah, who married her uncle Nahor, sibling to Abraham and Sarah, in a much more matrilocal context.

It is of interest that this particular episode in the text has provoked considerations concerning sexual propriety in Jewish tradition, per-haps reflecting an association between matrilocality and looseness of morality. Bethuel, Rebekah's father, who, according to tradition, wished to hinder Rebekah from going (Midrash: Genesis Rabba 60:12), is treated particularly badly. Legend suggests that Bethuel might have been responsible for the introduction of the *jus primae noctis*.[16] According to legend:

> Some say that among the Arameans a father would deflower his virgin daughter before her wedding; and that Bethuel, upon agreeing to Re-bekah's marriage, would have dishonoured her in this manner, had he not suddenly died. According to others, Bethuel, as King of Harran, claimed the sole right to deflower brides and, when Rebekah became nubile, the princes of the land gathered around, saying: "Unless Bethuel now treats his own daughter as he has treated ours, we shall kill them both!"[17]

Oddly enough, tradition suggests that he was called Bethuel as an allusion to the word BeTuLaH, which means virgin,[18] perhaps to suggest this activity on his part.

The traditional concern with Rebekah's virginity is also indicated by a legend that perhaps the servant Eliezer had sexual relations with her:

> When the travellers neared Hebron, Rebekah saw Isaac on his way back from Paradise, walking on his hands, as the dead do. She took fright, fell off her camel and was hurt by the stump of a bush. Abraham greeted her as he stood at the tent door, but said to Isaac: "Bondmen are capable of any deceit. Take this woman into your tent, and finger her to see whether she is still a virgin after this long journey in Eliezer's company!" Isaac obeyed and, finding Rebekah's maidenhead broken, sternly asked how this had come about. She answered: "My lord, I was frightened by your appearance, and fell to the ground, where the stump of a bush pierced

my thighs." "No, but Eliezer had defiled you!" cried Isaac. Rebekah, swearing by the Living God that no man had touched her, showed him the stump still wet with her virginal blood; and he believed at last. As for the faithful Eliezer, who had been near death because of a suspected crime, God took him alive into Paradise.[19]

Let us look at Rashi's commentary on the part of the text which says "and the girl was very good looking, a virgin, and no man had known her" (Genesis 24:16). With tradition, Rashi says that "virgin" refers specifically to "the place of virginity," namely, that the hymen had not been broken, alluding to the corresponding passage in the Midrash (Midrash: Genesis Rabba 60:5). The subsequent words "and no man had known her" mean that she was not involved in any sexual activity short of actual coitus. Rashi says, "not according to their custom. The daughters of the gentiles would guard the place of their virginity, but would have sex with other parts of their bodies. Which attests that she was clean of everything." Although the conclusion is that Rebekah was pure, it is peculiar that tradition found it necessary to even suggest that the plain meaning of the text needed qualification. Psychologically, the laying on of proofs suggests underlying doubt.

The question in tradition concerning Rebekah's purity, and the association of sexual looseness with matrilocality, may illuminate what has been regarded as one of the greatest mysteries in Rashi's writing. Genesis 28:5 says: "And Isaac sent Jacob away. And he went to Padan-aram, to Laban, the son of Bethuel the Aramean, the brother of Rebekah, the mother of Jacob and Esau." To the words "the mother of Jacob and Esau," Rashi provides a most unusual comment: "I do not know what it teaches us."

The mystery is why Rashi said, "I do not know what it teaches us." Nehama Leibowitz, in her commentary on Genesis, takes pains to point out this peculiarity in Rashi:

Many have praised Rashi for this display of humility and his literal fulfillment of one of the seven marks of the wise man outlined in *Pirke Avot* (V, 8): "regarding that which he has not understood he says, I do not understand it." But it behooves us to appreciate what Rashi was

driving at, as well as praise his intellectual modesty. The difficulty posed
by the text is quite obvious. What prompted the Torah to add the
apparently, completely superfluous fact, that Rebecca was the mother of
both Jacob and Esau? Surely the whole context of the sidra deals with
nothing else but the relations of Rebecca with "Esau her elder son" and
"Jacob her younger son." Rashi has taught us, on many other occasions,
that any descriptive word or phrase added in apposition to a familiar, and
already, fully defined term is not placed there for purely ornamental and
rhetorical reasons. It is meant to teach us something new. But Rashi
could find no purpose, didactic, informative, or otherwise, in the closing
words of our passage, and this is what the prince of commentators says
in so many words.

Why did Rashi see fit to proclaim to the world his failure to find a
plausible explanation of the superfluous text? Surely the admonition of
our Sages to "teach thy tongue to say, I do not know" was meant to apply
only in response to an inquiry. But no one was called upon gratuitously
to proclaim his ignorance. Surely Rashi has left many passages in the
Torah unexplained, and he could very well have passed over our text
without comment, since he had none to make. But this presents no
difficulty. Rashi left those texts unexplained which were so plain to him,
that he presumed they would be clear to any Torah student. If he had
remained silent, in our context, he would have been guilty of misrepre-
sentation, allowing scholars to imagine that everything was crystal clear,
failing to draw attention to a difficulty in the text. He therefore pro-
claimed to the world his failure to give an adequate explanation of the
final apposition, throwing out a challenge to commentators and scholars
to search, probe deeper and labour in their efforts to find their own
solution.[20]

I suggest, with perhaps foolish courage, that the meaning of
Rashi's mysterious "I do not know what it teaches us" can be found
in the story of Rebekah and the associated legends.

The story of Rebekah and the legends that it stimulated are
suggestive of matrilineality and looser norms of sexual behavior.
Rashi would have found such implications quite disagreeable. He
was certainly familiar with the legends and with the rabbinic commentaries on how, for example, Rebekah was raised among rogues
(Midrash: Genesis Rabba 63:4), protected her hymen, refrained

from unnatural immorality, and possibly lost her virginity through injury and thus was entitled to the virgin's 200 zuzim in a marriage settlement instead of the normal nonvirgin settlement of 100 zuzim (Midrash: Genesis Rabba 60:5).

It will be helpful to first consider how Rashi dealt with a parallel instance, "Rebekah, the mother of Jacob and Esau," which prompted the unusual disclaimer. To "And these are the generations of Isaac, Abraham's son; Abraham begat Isaac" (Genesis 25: 19), Rashi responds with a long commentary explaining the redundant phrase "Abraham begat Isaac." That phrase, he tells us, is intended to indicate that Abraham was truly the father of Isaac, because "the scoffers of the generation were saying, 'From Abimelech did Sarah conceive. Since she was with Abraham so many years and did not conceive from him.' " He proceeds to explain that the proof was that Isaac had features like Abraham.

Thus a similarly redundant "Rebekah, the mother of Jacob and Esau" should perhaps have elicited from Rashi some corresponding suggestion concerning the authenticity of parentage. He could not have been unaware of the legendary material that suggested that Rebekah may not have been a virgin when she married Isaac. Because the text does not repeat that Isaac was the father of Jacob and Esau, Rashi could characteristically have suggested that "the mother of Jacob and Esau" means that, although Rebekah was undoubtedly the mother of Jacob and Esau, Isaac may not have been the father. And this, of course, he could not bring himself to say. Thus, in his integrity, not quite able to pass over it without comment, and yet not wanting to throw doubt on the legitimacy of birth of Esau and Jacob, he wrote the unusual "I do not know what it teaches us," and leaves it, perhaps as Leibowitz suggests, for us to decipher.

MATRILOCALITY: JACOB, MOSES, AND LOT

A patent indication of matrilocality is to be found in the story of Jacob's stay at the household of his wives, Leah and Rachel, which is also the home of origin of his mother Rebekah and grandmother Sarah. We can understand this matter better by comparing it with

the story of Moses's stay at the household of his wife Zipporah and
the story of Lot's leaving Sodom. In each of these narratives there
are features that suggest a strong archaic matrilocal pull.

The story of Jacob's residing at the home of his wives begins with
Jacob's mother, Rebekah, saying to Isaac that she wishes that Jacob
would not take a wife locally: "I will be cut off from my kinsfolk
because of the Hittite daughters. If Jacob take a wife from the
Hittite daughters such as these, of the daughters of the land, why
do I have kinsfolk?"[21] (Genesis 27:46). Isaac dispatches Jacob to his
mother's home to take a wife from the daughters of Laban, his
mother's brother (Genesis 28:2).

On his departure, he receives a blessing from Isaac in the name
of El Shadai, which has been discussed above, as well as Elohim:

> And El Shadai bless you, and make you fruitful and multiply you, that
> you may be a congregation of peoples. And give you the blessing of
> Abraham, and to your seed with you; that you may inherit the land of
> your sojournings, which Elohim gave to Abraham (28:3–4).

On the way Jacob has a dream in which YHWH reaffirms the
promise of the land he is leaving and promises that he will see that
Jacob returns (28:13–15). On awakening, Jacob sets a pillar at the
place, and vows that, if Elohim will return him to his father's house,
he will give him a tithe (vs. 20–22). In this way the text strongly
indicates that, in spite of the jeopardy of permanent residence at the
household of his wives, he intends to return to his father's house.
In other words, in our interpretation God will guarantee that, in
spite of the matrilocal possibility, he will be returned to the patrilocal location.

On his arrival at Haran, Jacob encounters Rachel, his mother's
brother's daughter, at the well (29:9). Laban greets him as his bone
and flesh (29:14). At the end of a month Laban, Rachel's father and
Rebekah's brother, proposes that he be paid wages (vs. 14–15).
Jacob proposes that he serve for seven years and that in return he
be given Rachel as a wife (v. 18). Laban agrees (v. 19).

At the end of the period Laban tricks Jacob by putting Leah in
Rachel's place, and Jacob unwittingly has sexual relations with Leah,

thinking she is Rachel (v. 23). Jacob then serves for another seven years for Rachel (v. 28).

Jacob stays on for another six years negotiating and struggling with Laban over ownership of flocks that he might take with him on his departure. Getting the upper hand, Jacob arouses the resentment of Laban and his sons (31:1–2). YHWH then appears to Jacob and orders him to return to his paternal home (31:3). Jacob is reminded of the pillar and his vow (v. 13). He conspires with Rachel and Leah to leave. They are fearful that they might be cheated out of inheritance for themselves and their children (vs. 14–16). They take advantage of a temporary absence of Laban to escape. Rachel steals the teraphim.

Laban overtakes Jacob at Mount GiLaD (31:23). He chastises Jacob: "What have you done? And you have stolen my heart. And carried off my daughters as captives of the sword" (v. 26). Why did Jacob not allow Laban to send him off "with joy and songs, with tambourine and harp" (v. 27) and allow him "to kiss my sons and daughters?" (v. 29). And why did Jacob steal his gods? (v. 30).

Jacob invites Laban to search for the teraphim. Rachel deceives Laban by hiding the teraphim in a camel saddle she sits on, apologizing for not rising because "the manner of women" was upon her.

Jacob and Laban make a covenant and set up a pillar at the place, which the text names: "Therefore he [Laban] called the name of it GaLeiD and Mizpah" (vs. 48–49). They then go their respective ways.

It is interesting to note that there was some effort by those who added the pointing to the text to somehow distort the word GiLaD at this point (31:48). Vowels have been added to make it read GaLeiD, different than it is at 31:23 and elsewhere although the consonantal form is identical.

On a night just prior to Jacob's entry to Canaan, "a man wrestled with him, until the breaking of the dawn" (32:25) at the ford of Jabbok. He is touched on the thigh, and his name is changed to Israel.

Jacob "limps on his thigh" (32:32). He continues along slowly, "according to the pace of the cattle . . . and according to the pace of the children" (33:5). He arrives near Shechem in the land of Canaan and buys land (33:18–19).

Let us examine these verses. Rebekah's wish that her son take a matrilineal wife is clear. At the same time, there is evidence that the YHWH tradition is brought in by the authors to assert that Jacob is to return to his patrilocal home, which is affirmed by the setting up of a marker, the pillar.

The text clearly indicates that it is the wish of Laban that Jacob remain permanently in the matrilocal location. Although the women are coconspirators with Jacob in leaving the matrilocal location, nonetheless the text has Rachel stealing the teraphim.

If we accept the hypothesis that the teraphim mentioned in the text correspond to the numerous female figurines that have been uncovered in ancient Palestine, it is significant that they are characteristically legless. Psychological thought on artistic production suggests that the absence of legs on the teraphim might be indicative of a psychological disposition of nonmobility.[22] Thus the absence of legs on the female form of teraphim could be symbolic of nonmobile matrilocality. However, by virtue of Rachel's deception in the text, the text might be interpreted as asserting the triumph over matrilocality. The legless teraphim, symbolic of matrilocality, can indeed be carried from one place to another without loss.

It would appear that the teraphim were in some way related to claims. The story of Rachel's stealing of the teraphim is associated with Rachel's and Leah's fear that they would be deprived of their inheritance (31:14–16), and Jacob's fear that Laban would have sent him away "empty" (31:42).

The meaning of the stealing of the teraphim may be clarified by a story told in Judges. The landless Danites proceed on an expedition of conquest in order to acquire land. "In those days the tribe of Danites sought them an inheritance to dwell in" (Judges 18:1). The Danites pause at the house of Micah and steal the teraphim from him, an action analogous to stealing the teraphim from the house of Laban. After they make their conquest, they set up the stolen gods in the land they have taken.

I would suggest that the story of Jacob's all-night struggle is a remnant of a belief in a divine order that the male not leave his wife's location and a divine threat if he does. Jacob's encounter at the ford of Jabbok may help us understand the dynamic process involved in his reestablishing himself in his patrilocal location. Prior to the encounter Jacob sends his household ahead and remains behind (Genesis 32:23–24).

> And Jacob was left alone and a man wrestled with him until the rise of the dawn. And he saw that he could not prevail against him, and he touched the hollow of his thigh. And the hollow of Jacob's thigh was strained in the wrestling with him. And he said, "Send me away because the dawn is rising." And he said, "I will not let you go unless you bless me." And he said to him, "What is your name?" And he said, "Jacob." And he said, "No longer will your name be called Jacob, but Israel. For you have striven with Elohim and with men and you have prevailed." And Jacob asked and said, "Please tell me your name." And he said, "Why so do you ask for my name?" And he blessed him there. And Jacob called the name of the place Peniel; for I have seen Elohim face to face, and my soul is preserved. And the sun rose upon him as he passed over Peniel; and he limped on his thigh (Genesis 32:25–32).

Having deposited his wives in the patrilocal location, Jacob has now to engage in the last struggle with the remnant of matrilineality and matrilocality. They fight all night, and the one he is wrestling with cannot prevail against him. The victory is Jacob's. He needs release from the bond to the matrilocal location, and he needs the title, the blessing—where that blessing means the title, as in the blessing of Isaac in Genesis 27. And indeed he also gets his name changed to the name of the land, the patrilocal location, Israel. He has striven with God, the progenitor of his children and the one who could grant the title to the land, and he has won.

And he walks away with a limp. Claude Levi-Strauss's analysis of the Oedipus Complex is helpful in understanding the significance of the limp.[23] The struggle with God, and Jacob's winning that struggle, suggests that the Oedipus Complex might be relevant. Levi-Strauss observes that versions of the Oedipus myth characteristically entail some allusion to difficulties in walking straight and standing upright. Levi-Strauss says that "In mythology it is a univer-

sal characteristic of men born from the earth that at the moment
they emerge from the depth they either cannot walk or they walk
clumsily" (page 215). Limping and land are thus widely linked, and
in the Oedipus story they are associated with conflict over sexual
prerogative. In this saga, with Jacob's having overcome the matrilocal hold and arrived on the patrilocal location, he is endowed with
a trait that indicates a close association with the land. More prosai-
cally, though the total patriarchal saga starts with an address to
Abraham to walk—LeCH LeCHa (Genesis 12:1)—the authors
make the last of the three patriarchs lame on his rearrival at the
patrilocal land.

The story of Moses's leaving the home of his wife is similar in
some respects to the story of Jacob. Like Jacob, Moses leaves his
home and wanders until he meets the daughters of Reuel [Jethro]
at a well. He marries one of the daughters, Zipporah, and continues
to dwell in the matrilocal location (Exodus 2:15–22).

On Moses's journey from the matrilocal household, the text provides a fragment that has puzzled many critics and commentators:
"And it came to pass on the way at the lodging-place, that YHWH
met him, and sought to kill him. And Zipporah took a flint, and cut
off the foreskin of her son, and touched it to his feet; and she said:
'Because you are a bridegroom of blood to me.' So he let him alone.
Then she said: 'A bridegroom of blood in regard of the circumcision' " (Exodus 4:24–26).

Both the story of Jacob and the story of Moses suggest that
leaving the matrilocal location will be punished by the gods during
the journey. Such a remnant of divine threat may exist in the biblical
injunction that a man should leave his father and mother and cling
to his wife (Genesis 2:24). These two stories also indicate, however,
that the authors were trying to suggest a triumph over such a threat
associated with matrilocality, although the triumph was not without
some residual mark. In the one instance there is a thigh injury
associated with the confrontation; in the other it is the circumcision.
We might note, however, that thigh has been recognized as a euphemism for penis. Thus the swearing "under the thigh" of Abraham (Genesis 24:9) and Israel (47:29) has been interpreted as a

euphemism for the ancient custom of swearing on the genital organ.[24] And: "All the souls belonging to Jacob coming out of his thigh . . ." (Genesis 46:26); "All the souls coming out of the thigh of Jacob . . ." (Exodus 1:5); "And to Gideon there were seventy sons coming out of his thigh, for he had many wives" (Judges 8:30). Indeed, the suggestion is that castration could be the punishment for leaving and the circumcision indicates having overcome this jeopardy.

Jacob's setting up a pillar at his patrilocal location on leaving it and his being reminded of the pillar to terminate his stay at the matrilocal location strongly indicate that the pillar represents the tie to the patrilocal location. The second pillar, which the text associates with the words *Gilead* and *Mizpah,* set up in a departure covenant with Laban, indicates the conflict between matrilocality and patrilocality. We will understand this conflict better when we consider the Benjamin War in the next section.

THE BENJAMIN WAR

The occurrence of the words *Gilead* and *Mizpah* in the story of Jacob's overcoming the pull of matrilocality lead us to consider the Benjamin War, recounted in detail in the last three chapters of the book of Judges (19–21), and presumed to be part of the J document. Gilead and Mizpah signal the Benjamin War: "And all the children went out, and the congregation was gathered as one man, from Dan to Beersheba, and the land of Gilead, to YHWH of Mizpah" (Judges 20:1). It is reasonable to suppose that the account of the Benjamin War represents a real historical event, and that the story of Jacob's leaving the household of his wives and the story of Lot in Sodom were conditioned by the events associated with the Benjamin War.

The theme is conflict between matrilocality and patrilocality. A certain Levite living in Ephraim had a concubine, who came from the city of Bethlehem in Judah, who "whored on him and left him for her father's house in Bethlehem in Judah and was gone for four months" (Judges 19:2). The story thus begins with an allusion to a woman's assertion of her right to live in the matrilocal location. The text gives us no help in determining whether "whored on him" is meant literally or is intended as a metaphor for her mistreatment of him by leaving him. He goes after her to persuade her to return with him.

When he arrives in Bethlehem, she brings him to her father's house, and her father receives him with great hospitality. The father seeks to detain him in a manner quite parallel to the way in which Laban seeks to detain Jacob, cajoling and entreating, doing all that he can to keep him from leaving.

However, the man no longer allows himself to be persuaded to stay and proceeds to journey back to Ephraim with his concubine. To get to Ephraim he has to pass through Benjamin. He stops at the city of Gibeah, in Benjamin, where no one is willing to give him lodging. However, an Ephraimite living in Gibeah extends his hospitality to the Levite.

At this point the author introduces an episode very similar to the story of Lot in Sodom (Genesis 19:1 ff.). As they are eating and drinking in the house, "men of the city, men who were sons-of-Belial, surrounded the house, beat on the door and said to the man who was master of the house, the old man, saying, 'Bring out the man who came to your house, and we will know him'" (Judges 19:22). The owner of the house replies: "O, my brothers, I pray you, don't act so wickedly. After this man has come to my house, do not do this wicked thing. Here is my daughter, a virgin, and his concubine. I will bring them out now, and you can fuck[25] them, and do to them whatever is good in your eyes. But to this man don't do this wicked thing" (vs. 23–24). When they do not respond, "the man took his concubine and put her out in the street and they knew her and abused her all night until morning and released her at daybreak" (v. 25), to die on the doorstep.

If this is an earlier version of the Lot-Sodom, story we can understand the evil of Sodom as a violation of the emerging principle of patrilocality, an injury associated with an attempt to assert patrilocality.

The Levite divides the concubine's body into twelve pieces and sends the pieces "throughout all the borders of Israel" (v. 29) as a kind of call to arms, to defend the principle of patrilocality, which was not supported by the Benjamites.

The indignant warriors of Israel assemble at Mizpah (Judges 20:1 ff.). They demand that the culprits be delivered, but the Benjaminites refuse. The Israelites swear that "no man among us will give his daughter to Benjamin as a wife" (21:1). Let us say that this is a petulant reaction against Benjamin for their lack of honoring the patrilocal arrangements to which they have committed themselves.

A bitter battle rages for three days. Finally on the third day the Benjaminites are completed routed; the Israelites destroy the Benjaminites and burn all of their cities. However, six hundred men from Benjamin survive.

The Israelites repent the extensive devastation that they have wrought. They fear the possible loss of a total tribe of Israel. They are caught bv their vow that they would no longer provide wives from their tribes to the Benjaminites. How can they rectify the injury? They ascertain that the people of Jabesh-Gilead had not responded to the call to arms. They then kill the people of Jabesh-Gilead, sparing four hundred virgins. Here the word *Gilead* occurs, as it did in the Jacob departure episode: Mizpah the devastation in defense of patrilocality; Gilead the correction of the devastation of Benjamin and the affirmation of the principle of patrilocality by the movement of four hundred virgins to their husbands' homes. The Israelites take the virgins to Shiloh, which is in the territory of Ephraim, from which the Levite came originally. They arrange that these four hundred women from Jabesh-Gilead, and an additional number of women from Shiloh, become wives of the six hundred men remaining from Benjamin. The Benjaminites take their new wives and return "to their inheritance, and build the cities, and lived in them" (Judges 21:23).

Thus the Benjamin War may be interpreted as a story of victory over matrilocality. It is linked by theme to the Lot-Sodom story. It is linked to Jacob's departure from the matrilocal household by the words *Mizpah* and *Gilead* and the Laban-like behavior of the woman's father. And it asserts patrilocality by indicating that even the Benjaminites, the previous nonsupporters of patrilocality, are to follow patrilocality by moving women from elsewhere to Benjamin.

There are other hints that Gilead is linked to the conflict between matrilineality and patrilineality because it appears in a genealogy entailing the issue. The biblical genealogy makes Joseph (who himself lived in the land of his wife) the father of Manasseh and Ephraim. Machir is the son of Manasseh and Gilead the son of Machir. Gilead has six sons, one of whom is Shechem and another Hepher. Hepher is the father of Zelophehad (Numbers 26:28 ff.).

In the story of the Benjamin War there is a clear suggestion that Ephraim is associated with the belief in patrilocality. The Levite lives in Ephraim and would bring his concubine back to Ephraim. He is aided in Gibea by an Ephraimite. Gilead, on the other hand, who in this story refuses to fight for patrilocality, is the descendant of Manasseh. If Ephraim stands for patrilocality, and Manasseh stands for matrilocality, there is a possible explanation for why the authors included the story of Israel crossing his hands to place his right hand on Ephraim's head and left hand on Manasseh's (Genesis 48:13–14).

Matrilineal suggestions surround the name of Machir, the father of Gilead. Machir is the son of an Aramean concubine of Manasseh (I Chronicles 7:14). The text allows a reading that Machir married his sister Maacah (I Chronicles 7:15). In one of the genealogies descent from Machir is counted through his daughter (I Chronicles 2:21–24). We find an odd counting of genealogy through Gilead's sister as well: "These were the sons of Gilead the son of Machir, the son of Manasseh. And his sister Hammolecheth bore Ish-hod, and Abiezer, and Mahlah" (I Chronicles 7:17–18).

Shechem, the son of Gilead, is linked to a clear matrilineal base for warfare. After the death of Gideon (Jerubbaal), Abimelech, a son of Gideon by a concubine, returns to "Shechem to his mother's brothers . . . with all the family of the house of his mother's father" (Judges 9:1) and organizes them into an expedition against the children of Gideon's other wives (Judges 9:1 ff.). Abimelech enjoins them with, "remember also that I am your bone and your flesh" (Judges 9:2).

The name of Zelophehad, a grandchild of Gilead, is linked to the question of whether property is transmitted through daughters. Zelophehad had only daughters, and the question was raised as to whether they would inherit (Numbers 27:1 ff.). Elijah, too, comes from Gilead. I will indicate presently how one story of Elijah is linked to the classical notion of divine inpregnation and thus to matrilineality.

Matrilineal inheritance is indicated also in the story of Jephthah. "Jephthah the Gileadite . . . was the son of a whoring woman; and Gilead childed Jephthah. And Gilead's wife bore him sons; and when his wife's sons grew up, they drove out Jephthah, and said unto him: 'You shall not inherit in our father's house; for you are the son of another woman' " (Judges 11:1–2). It should also be pointed out that Jephthah addresses the elders of Gilead in Mizpah (Judges 11:11).

Gilead is linked with a husband taking the wife's family name: "the children of Barzillai, who took a wife of the daughters of Barzillai the Gileadite, and was called by their name" (Ezra 2:61–62; see also Nehemiah 7:63–64).

I suspect that those who added vowels to the text felt some nervousness over revealing the signal quality of the word *Gilead*. In two places they put vowels to Gilead to read as Galeed (Genesis 31:47, 48), although Rashi is at pains to indicate that Galeed and Gilead are the same.

NOTES

1. Kate Millett, *Sexual Politics* (Garden City, N. Y.: Doubleday and Company, 1970), pp. 51–54.
2. Mary Daly, "The Courage to See," *The Christian Century,* September 22, 1971, p. 1110.
3. A detailed table of analysis of Genesis by J, E, and P documents is found in the *Encyclopaedia Judaica,* Vol. 7, pp. 391–392 (Jerusalem: Keter Publishing House, 1972).
4. This verb is unambiguously transitive in the Hebrew.
5. Julian Morgenstern, "*Beena* marriage (Matriarchat) in ancient Israel and its

historical implications," *Zeitschrift für die Alttestamentische Wissenschaft,* 1929, *47,* 91–110; "Additional notes on *Beena* marriage (Matriarchat) in ancient Israel," *Zeitschrift für die Alttestamentische Wissenschaft, 49,* 46–58.

6. *Pirke De Rabbi Eliezer,* tr. Gerald Friedlander (New York: Benjamin Blom, 1971), pp. 272–73.

7. Stanley Rypins, *The Book of Thirty Centuries* (New York: Macmillan, 1951), p. 99.

8. Francis Brown, S. R. Driver, and Charles A. Briggs, *A Hebrew and English Lexicon of the Old Testament* (Oxford: Clarendon Press, 1975), p. 961.

9. Brown et al., pp. 961, 995.

10. *Orestes,* lines 552–554, in David Green and Richmond Lattimore (eds.), *The Complete Greek Tragedies. Euripides IV* (Chicago: University of Chicago Press, 1958), p. 145.

11. Raphael Patai, *The Hebrew Goddess* (New York: KTAV Publishing House, 1967), pp. 58–61.

12. Morgenstern, "Additional notes," pp. 51–52.

13. On another occasion where this form occurs—Genesis 13:3—Rashi makes no similar comment.

14. Mark Zborowski and Elizabeth Herzog, *Life Is with People* (New York: International Universities Press, 1952), p. 272.

15. Cuthbert A. Simpson, *The Early Traditions of Israel* (Oxford: Basil Blackwell, 1948), pp. 85–89. See also vs. 22:21, where the redactor substituted Bethuel for Laban; and 22:23, "And Bethuel begat Rebekah," was added by a later hand.

16. Louis Ginzberg, *The Legends of the Jews,* Vol. V (Philadelphia: Jewish Publication Society, 1954), p. 261.

17. Robert Graves and Raphael Patai, *Hebrew Myths: The Book of Genesis* (New York: McGraw-Hill, 1964), p. 185.

18. Ginzberg, p. 262.

19. Graves and Patai, p. 185.

20. Nehama Leibowitz, *Studies in the Book of Genesis,* tr. Aryeh Newman (Jerusalem: World Zionist Organization, 1972), pp. 286–287.

21. See pp. 85–86 above in connection with this translation.

22. Karen Machover, *Personality Projection in the Drawing of the Human Figure.* (Springfield, Ill.: Charles C. Thomas, 1949).

23. Claude Levi-Strauss, *Structural Anthropology,* tr. Claire Jacobson and Brooke Gruddfest Schoepf (New York: Basic Books, 1963), pp. 213 ff.

24. Gerhard Von Rad, *Genesis: A Commentary,* tr. John H. Marks (Philadelphia: Westminster Press, 1959), p. 249.

25. No euphemistic translation can do the Hebrew justice at this point. See Note 1, Chapter 8.

Divine Impregnation

The later patrilineally, patriarchically oriented authors of the Bible found the idea of God as a sexual being intolerable, and they sought to change it. Yet their modifications were not so complete as to remove all the traces of earlier meanings.

There are two major reasons for the incomplete censorship of divine impregnation. The first is that the great respect for the text inhibited too relentless a modification. The second is that a fundamental rationale for the idea of election by God is implicit in the idea of divine impregnation. Election by God meant descent from God, and that notion needed to be retained in some form. The idea of descent from gods was not rare in ancient times; indeed, this came to constitute one of the profound differences between Judaism and the subsequently developed Christianity. For the assertion of Christianity is that Jesus was "the only begotten Son" of God, the Father (John 1:18). The "only" is to be interpreted as negating the idea that all the Israelites were the offspring of God, as expressed, for example, in the Old Testament words of God to Moses: "And you should say to Pharaoh, So says YHWH, Israel is my firstborn son" (Exodus 4:22). Or, "I chose you the first-born of my cohabitation" (Isaiah 48:10).[1] In Christianity the view is that, while Jesus is the "only begotten Son," still he gave to those who received him "power to become the sons of God" (John 1:12).

In this chapter I will attempt to explicate some of the ways the theme of divine impregnation still resides in the text.

SONS OF GOD (ELOHIM)

Let us again consider the four verses describing how the sons of Elohim take wives from the daughters of men. Translated more literally than in Chapter 4, they are:

(1) And it was when the man began to become many on the face of the earth and daughters were born to them. (2) And the sons of Elohim saw the daughters of man that they were good and they took to themselves wives from whatever they chose. (3) And YHWH said my spirit shall not abide in man forever for in that he is flesh and his days shall be a hundred and twenty years. (4) The Nephilim were in earth in those days and also after that when came the sons of Elohim into the daughters of the man and they bore to them [children;] these same were the mighty of old men of name. (Genesis 6:1–4)

These verses are sandwiched in between the stories of creation, the genealogy of the patriarchs from Adam to Noah, Paradise, the Fall, and Cain and Abel, on the one hand; and the Flood, on the other.

The text is abrupt in that there is no transition to what precedes or succeeds it, although it has been suggested that these verses indicate the reason for the flood. It is generally held that the verses are from some independent source. One student describes them as a "cracked erratic boulder."[2] There is an opinion that at least three different hands were involved in producing the text we have.[3]

Modern translations—the Revised Standard Version, for example —follow the hypothesis that a scribal error changed YaDuR (abide in) to YaDoN (strive with) and have altered it in translation back to "abide in."[4] Rashi's comment clearly indicates "strive with," suggesting "wrathful and contentious." The Authorized (King James) Version has it as "strive with."

These four verses might be regarded as a kind of biblical version of a Freudian slip, a reminder and trace of repression. Slips, according to Freud, are indicative of deeper meanings behind the manifest expression. The sense of piety in those who recopied or reedited the text pressed them to leave things in. Thus there remain traces for us to decipher.

One classical interpretation of this passage is that the perpetrators of these wicked acts were fallen angels. The word *Nephilim* has the meaning of fallen ones. They were so called "because they fell and caused the world to fall," says Rashi. The fallen angel theme is elaborated in other versions of the story. Thus, for example, in I Enoch we have:

> And it came to pass when the children of men had multiplied that in those days were born unto them beautiful and comely daughters. And the angels, the children of the heaven, saw and lusted after them, and said to one another: "Come, let us choose us wives from among the children of men and beget us children." And Samiaza, who was their leader, said unto them: "I fear ye will not indeed agree to do this deed, and I alone shall have to pay the penalty of a great sin." And they all answered him and said: "Let us all swear an oath, and all bind ourselves by mutual imprecations not to abandon this plan but to do this thing." . . . And they were in all two hundred. . . . And these are the names of their leaders: Samiaza, their leader . . . and Aasel." (I Enoch 6:1–8)

Another interpretation is that they are not the sons of God at all. Rabbi Simon ben Yochai was so adamant on this point that he cursed all who would call them "sons of Elohim" (Midrash: Genesis Rabba, 26:5). One of the commentators, Rabbi Judan, evidently disturbed by the fact that the women might have given their consent to this kind of activity, attempted to read out of the word *fair* in verse 2 an interpretation that would have mitigated their responsibility in the matter. He alluded to the *jus primae noctis,* the right of a nobleman to have sexual intercourse with a bride on the first night. The text should have been written, he said, " 'When they were made fair.' When they were making her fair, adorned to enter the bridal canopy, one of the nobles would come in and claim her first" (Rashi, ad locum, from Midrash: Genesis Rabba, 26:5). In order to squeeze this rather remote interpretation out of it, Rabbi Judan found it necessary to claim that the text was defective. Claiming that the text is defective is characteristically done only with very strong reason. Other elaborations suggest that the angels were victims of the seductive actions of the women: "The angels who fell from their holy place in heaven saw the daughters of the generations of Cain walking about naked, with their eyes painted like harlots, and they went astray after them, and took wives from amongst them. . . ."[5] So low and obscene is the activity suggested in these verses that "of all which they chose" is said to mean that they had sexual intercourse not only with women, but with animals as well (Rashi, ad locum).

Taken together, these interpretations suggest a common mechanism of denial, an attempt to strengthen a denial by the multiplication of justifications at the expense of consistency. It is reminiscent of the story of the man who was asked by a neighbor to return a borrowed pot. The man replied that he did not borrow it, that it was broken when he borrowed it, and that he had already returned it. Analogously, it is asserted that the text is defective, they were not angels in the first place, they were fallen angels anyway, the women were forced into it, the males were seduced by the females, what they did was worse even than what the text says, and it was all justified by God in destroying them in the succeeding story of the Flood. Nevertheless, the theme of divine impregnation seems undeniable in these verses.

THE DIVINE VISITATION

The blatant assertion of divine impregnation in Genesis 6:1–4 may be understood as a harbinger of and preparation for the birth of Isaac. That story is, of course, basic for the meaning of the remainder of the text, both Old and New Testaments. Genesis 6:1–4 may also be seen, together with the story of the birth of Isaac, as an example of theme-splitting, with what is veiled in Genesis 18 expressed more openly in Genesis 6:1–4.

The birth of Isaac is a central myth basic to the ideologies of Judaism, Christianity and Islam. The story of the divine visitation to Abraham and Sarah is contained in the eighteenth chapter of Genesis, to which we now turn our attention.

Translating the text of Genesis 18:1–19 with greater attention to literalness than to literary quality, we have:

(1) And YHWH appeared to him by the oaks of Mamre. And he was sitting in the door of the tent in the heat of the day.

(2) And he raised his eyes and he saw and here three men standing over him. And he saw and he ran to meet them from the door of the tent and bowed to the earth.

(3) And he said Adonai if now I have found favor in your eyes do not I pray you pass from on your servant.

(4) Let now a little water be fetched and wash your feet and recline under the tree.

(5) And I will fetch a morsel of bread and stay your hearts. Afterward you will pass on, for as much have you come to your servant. And they said so do as you have said.

(6) And Abraham hurried to the tent to Sarah and said quick up three measures of fine meal knead it and make cakes.

(7) And to the herd ran Abraham and took a son-of-the-herd tender and good and gave it to the boy and he hurried to make it.

(8) And he took butter and milk and the son-of-the-herd which he had made and gave it before them and he stood over them under the tree and they ate.

(9) And they said *to him* where is Sarah your wife and he said here in the tent.

(10) And he said I will return I will return to you at the time of lifing and here will be a son to Sarah your wife and Sarah heard at the door of the tent and he was behind it.

(11) And Abraham and Sarah were old people coming into days it ceased to happen to Sarah the manner of women.

(12) And Sarah laughed in herself saying after I have waxed old will pleasure occur to me and Adonai is old.

(13) And YHWH said to Abraham why this did Sarah laugh saying will I truly child and I have become old.

(14) Is anything too difficult from YHWH? At the time I will return to you at the time of lifing and to Sarah a son.

(15) And Sarah denied saying I did not laugh because she was afraid and he said no but you laughed.

(16) And the men rose from there and looked toward Sodom and
      Abraham walked with them to send them.
(17) And YHWH said shall I hide from Abraham what I am
      doing?
(18) And Abraham will be will be a large nation and mighty and
      in him will be blessed all the nations of the earth.
(19) For I have known him in order that he command his sons
      and his house after him and they keep the way of YHWH
      to do righteousness and justice in order that YHWH bring
      on Abraham what he said to him.

The indications are that this passage is of J origin because of the
use of YHWH throughout, and typical J expressions in it. According to Simpson, J_2 substituted verses 10–15 for J_1's account at this
point.[6]

This chapter contains an instance of dotted words in the Hebrew
manuscripts. Such dots are a major signal to the reader to be careful
in taking the words of the text as authentic. The dots appear over
the word for "to him" in verse 9. Altogether there are fifteen such
dotted places in the Bible, ten in the Pentateuch. Five of them are
in Genesis, three in the Abraham narrative (16:5, 18:9, 19:33). Such
dots have been interpreted as a signal that the text is defective. The
meaning of the dots is indicated as follows: "Thus said Ezra [the
presumptive original compositor]: 'If Elijah (the prophet) should
come and say to me, why did you write [these doubtful words] in
this manner? I will answer him: I have already dotted them. But if
he should say: You have written them correctly, I shall remove the
dots from them.' "[7]

Interestingly enough, the classical interpretation of the dots at
this point is that they indicate that the angels communicated with
Sarah as well as with Abraham, since the particular dotted letters
make "where is he?" indicating that the angels inquired of her
concerning her husband (Rashi, ad locum; BT, Nezikin: Baba Mezia
87a).

Rashi's commentary to verse 13 indicates openly that the text has
been changed:

Will I truly. Is it really true that I will child? *And I have become old.*
The written text altered in the interests of peace. What she actually said
was "and my lord is old."

Thus Rashi would lead us to understand both that Sarah may not
be as old as it appears and that the text may have been tampered with
for the sake of peace.

On the manifest level the story is that both Abraham and Sarah
were old people, and that angels came to announce to them that, in
spite of their great age, they would have a child. Yet there are
accounts in the text, both before and after the eighteenth chapter
of Genesis, which suggest that both Abraham and Sarah are less than
infertile or senile at the time of this divine visitation. There is a prior
narrative of Abraham's having a child with Hagar (Genesis 16) and
a subsequent one of his having children with Keturah (Genesis 25),
allowing him to be quite fertile in the part of the narrative of Genesis
18. Similarly, the text provides both a prior and a subsequent story
of Sarah's physical and sexual attractiveness. In the first she is found
attractive enough to be taken into the harem of Pharaoh (Genesis
12), and in the second attractive enough to be taken into the harem
of Abimelech (Genesis 20).

There is some scholarly opinion that the allusions to the age of
Sarah, as well as other chronological indications, were entered into
the text at a considerably later date—in the fifth century, by the P
author. Von Rad says "we must imagine [Sarah] as still young in
contrast with the Priestly (P) chronology. . . ."[8]

THE CAKES AND EATING

There is the matter of the absent cakes at the banquet served by
Abraham. In verse 5 Abraham says that he will "fetch a morsel of
bread." In verse 6 he gives Sarah instruction to prepare cakes for the
meal. In verse 7, Abraham leaves Sarah quite alone with the guests
while he busies himself with the slaughtering, butchering, and cooking of a calf. When he serves the meal in verse 8, the cakes are
conspicuously missing. Why did Sarah not prepare cakes as she was

requested? The classical explanation is that Sarah must have become menstruous. According to the rabbinical laws of Niddah,[9] the dough was unclean, and therefore not served, as Rashi indicates. The absurdity of this explanation is clear, as the rabbinical rules were made long after the presumptive time of this episode. Indeed, Rashi does not even try to explain Abraham's serving of meat and dairy products together, which is also in violation of subsequently developed rabbinical laws.

A more parsimonious reading of the text is that Sarah was otherwise occupied. The authors and editors of the text must have had some notion of about how long Abraham's preparations should take. Although the text does not directly indicate any conversation between Sarah and the guests, nonetheless, as has been pointed out, such contact is suggested by classical interpretation of the dotted word.

The Talmud brings to mind a psychoanalytic type of interpretation that some divine event took place between the time that Abraham ran to the herd and his serving of the food, as indicated by an interspersion into the biblical text concerning Abraham's leaving his guests near the tent with Sarah. The biblical text itself reads "And to the herd ran Abraham and took a son-of-the-herd tender and good and gave it to the boy and he hurried to make it. And he took butter and milk . . ." (Genesis 18:7–8). In the Talmud this is quoted with an interspersion from Numbers, "And a wind went out from YHWH" (11:31) as follows: "And to the herd ran Abraham—and a wind went out from YHWH—and he took butter and milk . . ." (BT, Nezikin: Baba Mezia 86b).

The idea of wind's having a divine effect is not strange to tradition, not least because the world for wind and spirit are the same.

The idea of wind as coming from the divine is to be found in the New Testament:

> And suddenly a sound came from heaven like the rush of a mighty wind, and it filled all the house where they were sitting. And there appeared to them tongues as of fire, distributed and resting on each of them. And

they were all filled with the Holy Spirit and began to speak in other tongues, as the Spirit gave them utterance (Acts 2:2–4).

The probability that the Talmudic authors may have been signalling a sexual contact between YHWH and Sarah is strengthened somewhat if we compare John Allegro's hypothesis about the meaning of wind from YHWH, and assume that this understanding was available to the authors of the Talmud in some way. Allegro writes: "The most forceful spurting of this 'seed' is accompanied by thunder and a shrieking wind. This is the 'voice' of God. Somewhere above the sky a mighty penis reaches an orgasm that shakes the heavens. The 'lips' of the penis-tip, the glans, open, and the divine seed shoots forth and is borne by the wind to earth."[10]

The abiding symbolism of baking cakes, as Sarah was enjoined to do, is made evident in Vance Packard's report of some years ago on motivational research in the advertising industry. He reports on a study by James Vicary of cake symbolism that

> concluded that "baking a cake traditionally is acting out the birth of a child" so that when a woman bakes a cake for her family she is symbolically presenting the family with a new baby, an idea she likes very much. Mr. Vicary cited the many jokes and old wives' tales about cake making as evidence: the quip that brides whose cakes fall obviously can't produce a baby yet; the married jest about "leaving a cake in the oven"; the myth that a cake is likely to fall if the woman baking it is menstruating. A psychological consulting firm in Chicago also made a study of cake symbolism and found that "women experience making a cake as making a gift of themselves to their family," which suggests much the same thing.[11]

I do not imagine that the author of the advertising jingle, "Nothin' says lovin', like somethin' from the oven—and Pillsbury says it best," was directly informed by biblical exegesis.

In the eighth verse there occurs what appears to be a harmless phrase to the effect that, while Abraham stood by after serving the food, the angels ate it: "and they ate." This occurs immediately prior to the inquiry concerning the whereabouts of Sarah, "where is Sarah your wife?" Strangely enough, the classical rabbinical interpretation at this point is to deny the plain meaning of the text, to deny that the angels ate, to hold the text in error, in spite of the manifest clarity of the text. Summarizing rabbinical opinion, Rashi says that they only appeared to be eating (Midrash: Genesis Rabba 48:14; BT, Nezikin: Baba Mezia 86b).

Why should the commentators deny the plain meaning of the text? It is true that angels are supposed to have clean bowels (BT, Moed: Yoma 30a). However, I suggest another possible reason—the commentators were aware that, at least in some unconscious sense, eating is a euphemism for coitus. The psychoanalytic literature has interpreted eating as coitus in the story of Adam and Eve in the Garden of Eden.[12] Thus in order to put an interpretive fence around the story, to discourage the reading of "and they ate" as indicating that the visitors engaged in coitus, it became important to deny that the visitors ate.

SARAH'S VIRTUE

That Sarah is telling a lie is on the manifest level of the text. Allowing the meaning of "laugh" to be making a certain sound of mirth, we find that she laughed (vs. 12, 13), denied that she laughed, and was confronted with her denial (v. 15). Because the author allows an attribution of a lie to Sarah, it may be valuable to consider the psychodynamics of lying. In a previous work in which I dealt with the psychology of secrets, I pointed out that a person seeking to hide something may be inclined to confess to some lesser violation in order to give the impression of being sincere.[13] Some similar psychology may have been operating in the minds of the composers or editors of the text. By allowing Sarah the manifest failing of being a liar, they seek to conceal an even greater offense.

Von Rad refers to Sarah's lie as "audacious."[14] In point of fact, it is not very audacious in context. The composers of the text do not appear to consider telling a lie very heinous. We can compare Sarah's lie with Abraham's lies on two occasions about the fact that

Sarah is his wife (Genesis 12 and 20). What is attributed to Sarah here is more in the way of suggesting some domestic discord than an "audacious lie." Indeed, according to Jewish law, women are disqualified generally from giving testimony as witnesses in legal proceedings (BT, Shebuot 30a; Baba Kamma 88a),[15] "for even one of the best of them, Sarah, attempted to tell an untruth."[16]

If the word *laugh* here is intended in the sexual sense (see pp. 118–119), then the deceit suggested is more serious. Ironically, in Philo's allegorical scheme, Sarah is taken to be Virtue; and Martin Luther, in his commentary to the text at this point, celebrated Sarah's virtue for pages, laying out a vision of her conscientious attention to housewifely duties and paying little attention to the text's clear indication that she did not serve her guests with food.

Sarah is hardly presented as a person of great virtue. Her behavior with respect to Hagar and Ishmael—on the one hand, offering Hagar to Abraham to have a child with, and, on the other, twice seeking to destroy Hagar (Genesis 16:6 ff and 21:10 ff)—is outrageous. Indeed, according to tradition, Sarah should have reached the same old age that Abraham did, but forty-eight years were taken off her life because she said to Abraham in her speech of resentment against Hagar, "Let YHWH judge between me and you" (Genesis 16:5, Midrash: Genesis Rabba 45:5). Tradition also added details to Sarah's abuse of Hagar, such as slapping her, restraining her from further cohabitation, and making her carry water buckets and towels to the baths (Midrash: Genesis Rabba 45:6). I would suggest, however, that depiction of Sarah as a less than virtuous person serves to prepare the reader for the possibility that she would engage in other less than virtuous acts.

Furthermore, there are indications that sexual purity is not held at such high value by the authors of the narrative. For example, in Genesis 12:9–20 from J, Sarai and Abram (their names not yet changed to Sarah and Abraham) journey into Egypt. Abram addresses Sarai with the words: "Here now, I know that you are a good-looking woman. And it will be that the Egyptians will see you and they will say, 'This is his wife.' And they will kill me and keep you alive. Say, I pray, that you are my sister, in order that it may be good for me because of you, and that my soul will live on your account" (Genesis 12:11–13).

Following this exchange, the narrative continues with: "And it was when Abram came to Egypt and the Egyptians saw the woman, that she was very pretty. And the princes of Pharaoh saw her and hailed her to Pharaoh and the woman was taken into the house of Pharaoh" (12:14–15).

Thus, clearly, the contributors of this narrative would have us understand that allowing a female from one's household to reduce jeopardy by her sexual conduct is hardly objectionable. The notion of protective gallantry with respect to women's virtue, an essential feature of a more mature patrilineality, is yet to be developed.

A similar message appears in the story of Lot. When the Sodomites are clamoring at the door of Lot's house that he surrender his guests to them, the biblical authors ascribe to Lot the following—seemingly noble, yet ungallant—offer to the Sodomites: "Here now, I have two daughters who have not known a man. Let me, I pray you, bring them out to you; and you may do to them whatever is good in your eyes. Only don't do anything to these men" (Genesis 19:8).

The Lot story, which follows directly on the divine visitation to Abraham, clearly indicates that hospitality is of higher value than the sexual purity of women in a household. What is thus communicated is that sexual exclusiveness is not a paramount value. This message could clarify the implication that Sarah might not be engaging in a heinous activity, for Sarah would have been offered in hospitality as were the daughters of Lot. In this sense, the Lot story that follows may be regarded as a commentary on what was suggested by the preceding chapter: that hospitality is a greater virtue than sexual purity.

IDENTITY VIOLATIONS

Mutiple violations of the principle of identity prevail in this brief narrative. The actors are Abraham, Sarah, a boy, and visitors. Yet it is difficult to identify them precisely in the course of the narrative.

I suggest that these identity violations serve a purpose. The text signals to the reader that presumed identity may be wrong in any situation, and thus raises the question of the identity of the male progenitor in conception. Let us enumerate some of these violations of identity:

1. In verse 1 YHWH appears in the singular. In verse 2 *three* men are mentioned.

2. In verse 2 Abraham is said to note three *men*. At the beginning of the succeeding chapter it says "And two *angels* came to Sodom in the evening" (19:1). It is clear from the context that these are the same actors. Thus a conflation of the characteristics of men and angels is suggested. If we allow that the main subject of the narrative is conception, and recognize that the text has already more explicitly indicated that the "sons of Elohim" may have sexual intercourse with the "daughters of men," it is possible that this has occurred here; that these angels do what men do.

3. There are *three* men (18:2) and *two* angels (19:1), a clear violation of identity in numbers. Rashi's interpretation is revelatory here. Rashi says (ad locum 18:2): "one to inform Sarah, and one to destroy Sodom, and one to heal Abraham. For one angel does not carry out two errands." Yet in the rendering of this explanation, Rashi immediately signals a message to refute what he has just said: "Raphael who healed Abraham went from there to rescue Lot," indicates that what he had just said about angels not carrying out more than one errand was false, and thus allows the suggestion of other errands to be performed. We may believe either that Rashi was confused or that he was leaving a signal to the reader to read more carefully—there was yet another errand to be performed.

It is valuable at this point to draw attention to the problem of writing in the face of political or religious opposition. Leo Strauss has said that "If a master of the art of writing commits such blunders as would shame an intelligent high school boy, it is reasonable to assume that they are intentional. . . ."[17] Rashi is certainly a master. So such a patent contradiction may well have been intentional.

4. The use of the word aDoNaY actually spelled out in two of the verses cited suggests that the authors were attempting to signal an alternative message.

The way in which the word aDoNaY has been used throughout Jewish tradition bears on this. In every instance in which the name YHWH appears, the pious read it aloud as aDoNaY, in deference to the biblical commandment that the name of God must not be taken in vain. Literally, aDoNaY means "my Lord." In the passage cited, the word aDoNay, spelled out as such, appears in verse 3 as an address to the visitors. Rashi interprets this as being "lord" in both the holy and profane sense. Targum Onkelos, the classical Aramaic version of the Bible, renders the word with the usual abbreviation of YHWH, YY. Thus the word is introduced in a way that leaves the meaning ambiguous.

The word appears again in Sarah's speech in verse 12, referring to Abraham, and appears to be used in the sense of "my husband." Targum Onkelos translates this in the profane sense by the use of RiBoNY instead of the abbreviation for YHWH. Indeed, the word has had vowels attached to it in a manner that would stress the profane meaning of the word; yet, it must be pointed out that the earlier text does not contain vowels, and that the vowels are a much later addition. The end result is to create an ambiguity of identity between YHWH and Abraham in connection with the conception by alluding to both with the word Adonai, which, conveniently, has both profane and nonprofane meanings. Interestingly, Philo interpreted the word in verse 12 as referring to God.

5. In verse 3 Abraham uses the singular form of address. In verse 4 he is clearly addressing more than one, as the words for "wash your feet" are second person plural. In verses 5 and 9 the visitors are plural. In verse 10 the speaker is singular. In verse 13 it is YHWH who speaks in the singular. In verse 14 the speaker of the words "I will return" is singular. Interestingly enough, rabbinical interpretation of verse 13 attributes the last phrase, "I have become old," seemingly alluding to Sarah as old, to YHWH, with the interpretation that God has been challenged on the basis of his age! Thus, in the Midrash we have the following statement attributed to God: "You declare yourselves young and your companions old, yet I am too old to perform miracles" (Midrash: Genesis Rabba 43:16). In this way even the Midrash hints at God's procreative powers with

respect to Sarah, taking the suggestion of virile senility to be descriptive of God and thus requiring denial by the Midrashic source. Thus the rabbinical interpreters are confused about the identity of the visitors with Abraham and even ascribe the problem of age and sexual senility to God!

The identity of the speaker to Sarah in verse 15 is indeterminate, except that the verb is singular and masculine. It could be Abraham, as is commonly understood when it is read as a bit of domestic discord, with Sarah as liar. An interpretation of the identity of the speaker is forced on the translator into English, who must decide on whether to capitalize the word "he" in "he said" of verse 15. If it is God who is the speaker, then one capitalizes. The older King James did not capitalize, thus making the speaker Abraham: "And he said, Nay; but thou didst laugh." The Jewish Publication Society translation of 1916, however, clearly opted for God as the speaker: "And He said: 'Nay; but thou didst laugh.' " Interestingly, the Revised Standard Version defers the decision by starting a new sentence, so that one does not know whether the capitalization is grammatical, from the beginning of the sentence, or indicative of God: "He said, 'No, but you did laugh.' " In its commentary to verse 15, the Midrash has it quite explicitly according to several sages that God never conversed directly with a woman except Sarah, when he spoke to her saying, "No, but you did laugh" (Midrash: Genesis Rabba 48:20).

The confusion in the text has allowed varieties of interpretations of the identity of the visitors. One interpretation is that YHWH is accompanied by two angels (Jerusalem Bible). Augustine suggests that "some think that one of them was Christ." Another interpretation is that God came together with three angels (Rashbam, Ibn Ezra, and Nachmanides; *Pirke De Rabbi Eliezer,* p. 179). The early Church interpreted the three visitors as the Holy Trinity (Von Rad, p. 201).

Tradition indicates that the angels were Michael to bring the tidings of Isaac to Sarah, Raphael to heal Abraham, and Gabriel to overturn Sodom (BT, Nezikin: Baba Mezia 86b). Michael's achievement is said to be greater than Gabriel's (BT, Zeraim: Berakoth 4b). It was Michael who protected Isaac from Abraham's knife (Ginzberg, I, p. 201). If Michael is the angel associated with the birth of Isaac, it is appropriate that he rescue Isaac from his jeopardy.

LAUGHTER AND *IN HERSELF*

Consider verse 12: "And Sarah laughed in herself saying after I have waxed old will pleasure occur to me and adonai is old?"

Consider: "And Sarah laughed in herself." In Hebrew this is VaTiZCHaK SaRaH BeKiRBaH (Va = and; TiZCHaK = laugh; SaRaH = Sarah; Be = in; and KiRBaH = herself.)

The word *laugh* also means coitus as a transitive verb. This usage is unambiguous in Genesis 26:8, "And behold Isaac was laughing Rebekah his wife." The meaning is quite clear in the story of Potiphar's wife's charge that Joseph sought a sexual relationship with her: "The Hebrew slave came to me, whom you brought to us, to laugh me" (Genesis 39:17). Rashi specifically indicates the sexual meaning of the word (ad locum, 26:8).

Now consider KiRBaH, herself. It also means womb. This usage is clear in Genesis 25:22, "And the sons struggled in the womb." Isaac's name means coitus, while the consonantal name of his wife, RBKH, is an anagram of KiRBaH.

Rashi's comment strongly points to a physical interpretation of the word KiRBaH. "BeKiRBaH. She looked at her belly and she said, 'Is it possible that these inwards [KeRaBaYiM, the plural of KiRBaH] shall bear a child' " (Rashi, ad locum, 18:12).

If we put these meanings together, instead of "And Sarah laughed in herself," we have rather, "And he laughed Sarah in her womb," in the transitive and sexual sense. Remember that Isaac's name means coitus in the transitive sense, and Isaac's wife's name, RiBKaH, is an anagram of KiRBaH. Thus Isaac's marriage to Rebecca is parallel to "And he laughed Sarah in her womb," in this verse.

There are, however, two grammatical objections to consider. The first is that Hebrew characteristically calls for a prefix, 'eT, before a noun as the object of a verb. This is lacking before "Sarah." However, this usage is not without exception. It does not occur, for example, in 17:24, as Rashi points out. The purpose of leaving out the eT, according to Rashi, is to qualify the truth of what is being asserted. If we apply this explanation to the missing eT before "Sarah" in verse 12, then the absence of the eT qualifies the truth of what appears to be asserted there.

Another explanation of a missing eT for the accusative is that there is an alternate archaic Hebrew form for indicating the object of a verb, placing an aH ending on an object noun. This archaic form still exists in the text.[18] Sarah's name conveniently provides this, as it already has the aH ending. It is even remotely possible that one purpose of the change of Sarah's name from Sarai was to allow Sarah to be the object of the verb in this case.

It is true, however, that the verb *laugh* has a grammatical form to indicate a female rather than a male subject. To complete our hypothesis we would have to surmise that, if the text was more explicit at any time, it has been changed, as so many similar changes have taken place in the textual history. Indeed, as has been previously indicated, the scribal tradition did allow changing a single letter and changes to remove obscenity.

There is further evidence bearing on the distortion of the meaning of KiRBaH in verse 12 in the history of the Septuagint. The Talmud contains an account of the translation and especially of how certain deliberate errors were made.

According to this account King Ptolemy of Egypt brought together seventy-two Jewish elders, placed each in a room by himself, and ordered each of them, "Write me the Torah of Moses your master." Each translated, and each, under God's prompting, made certain deliberate errors. The Talmud lists these deliberate errors. God prompted all the scholars to translate verse 12 as "And Sarah laughed among her relatives," which requires reading *KiRBaH* (womb) as *KRuBiYaH* (relatives) (BT, Moed: Megillah). The reason for the distortion by the translators from the Hebrew into the Greek may have been to conceal the alternative meaning I have suggested.

Let us now consider "after I have waxed old" of verse 12. The consonantal text translated as "waxed old" is BLTY. With vowels added it can be either BLoTiY, meaning become old or worn out, after the verb BLH; or BiLTiY, which would mean my deprivation, from the particle of negation BLT.[19] BLTY pointed as BiLTiY occurs around 120 times in the Old Testament. It is pointed as BLoTiY only once, and only in 18:12![20] Thus it is a unique pointing. If we allow the characteristic pointing, the whole phrase then becomes "After my deprivation will pleasure happen to me and my lord is old?" It thus suggests her reaction to a sexual opportunity to compensate for a life with an aging husband.

The word that is commonly translated as pleasure, eDNaH, in Genesis 18:12 is related to Eden. It has connotations characteristically associated with Paradise. In Tyndale's early English translation the word was translated as lust. Moffatt translated the word as marriage bliss; the Vulgate, as *voluptum.*

Septuagint authors translated BLTY as though it was pointed in the characteristic fashion as BiLTY, rendering Sarah's remark as "The thing has not yet happened to me. . . ." However, the Septuagint deletes any translation of eDNaH. Thus the authors of the Septuagint attempted to cover the seeming obscenity by refraining from translating eDNaH, while translating BLTY as in the rest of the text; while the editors who added points to the Hebrew text attempted to cover up the meaning by a unique pointing of BLTY, leaving eDNaH! Evidently, both the scribes who added points to the Hebrew text and the translators into Greek were motivated to cover what appeared to them to be an obscenity. They chose different methods to achieve the same end. Philo must have had an earlier less censored version of the Septuagint, as his citation included a translation of eDNaH, whereas later versions of the Septuagint do not.[21]

THE ANGEL IN THE TENT

Manifestly Sarah is inside the tent during the visitation, and there is no communication between her and the visitors except for her eavesdropping on the conversation that takes place outside the tent. As indicated, however, the rabbinical tradition refutes this lack of contact on the basis of the dotted word, which was taken to indicate that the angels at least inquired of Sarah concerning her husband Abraham. Indeed, as I mentioned earlier, legend has it that Sarah was the only woman that God ever spoke to.

Consider the strong hospitality theme in the text. The chapter opens by telling us that Abraham was sitting in the opening of the tent "in the heat of the day" (Genesis 18:1), suggesting that the best place to be in the heat is in the shade of the tent. Rashi tells us that Abraham was looking for passersby "who he might take *into his house*" (ad locum, 18:1). Yet Abraham does not invite the visitors into his house but suggests that they recline under the tree (18:4). When he serves the meal they are *under the tree* (18:8). Presumably they are outside the tent, and Sarah inside, as further indicated by "And they said to him, 'Where is Sarah your wife?' And he said: 'Here, in the tent.' " Philo, however, is loose with the text and has the guests entertained inside, where Sarah is, rather than outside the tent.[22]

The simplest rendering of the last two words of verse 10, VeHu aCHaRaV would be simply, "and he behind."[23] It would easily suggest that Sarah had a companion with her in the tent. The Targum Pseudo-Jonathan identifies that companion as Ishmael. "And Sarah was listening in the tent door, and Ishmael was standing behind her and noted what the angel said."[24] The Revised Standard Version has it "Sarah was listening at the tent door behind him." Rashi says that "The door was behind the angel." The Samaritan text has "and she behind." Simpson interprets the Samaritan text to mean that she was behind the tent door.[25] Philo says, "And Sarah heard, for she was by the entrance of the tent behind him."[26] Von Rad interprets the Septuagint as "the door of the tent was 'behind him' (i.e., Yahweh)"; and he interprets the Hebrew text as "Sarah was 'behind it,' (i.e., the door of the tent)."[27] Sandmel interprets the Septuagint to mean that Sarah was behind Abraham.[28]

Thus we have a variety of texts, translations, and interpretations of this phrase. Behind it all is the simple and obvious suggestion that

Sarah had a visitor in the tent with her, which the texts, translations, and interpretations seek to disguise.

Philo explicitly read the text as indicating that Isaac was the result of divine impregnation of Sarah.

Philo was born around 20 B.C. and lived in Alexandria, a major center of the Jews in dispersion as well as a major center of Hellenistic culture. The main thrust of his work was to combine the two cultures. He appears to have written all of his commentary from the Greek Septuagint and to have known little if any of the original Hebrew.

We must consider Philo's general approach to appreciate how it was possible for him to have overcome the resistance characteristic of other commentators. Philo interprets biblical characters allegorically. Thus Sarah was Virtue, Abraham was Teaching, Isaac was Joy, and so on. Armed, as it were, with his allegorical interpretation, which disallowed or denigrated an historical interpretation, Philo could be explicit without the reluctance that came with taking the text literally. Thus to allow that Isaac was the product of divine impregnation was for him to add only a further allegorical element, not a possible aspersion on the presumptive ancestors.

In Philo's presentation there is little ambiguity that Sarah was impregnated by God. Out of this union came Isaac, Joy, which was then presented as a gift to Abraham. The meaning of Abraham's move to sacrifice Isaac is that it demonstrates Abraham's readiness to offer Joy back to God (VI, 101).

Philo indicates that ". . . we must hold Isaac to be not a product of created beings, but a work of the uncreated One. For if 'Isaac' means 'laughter,' and according to Sarah's unerring witness God is the maker of laughter, God may with perfect truth be said to be Isaac's father" (II, 285).

Referring to Genesis 21:6, where Sarah says "God made laughter to me," Philo says, "Therefore, O ye initiate, open your ears wide and take in the holiest teachings. The 'laughter' is joy, and 'made' is equivalent to 'beget,' so that is what is said of this kind, the Lord begat Isaac. . ." (I, 451). The text, he says, "shows us Sarah conceiving at the time when God visited her in her solitude (Genesis 21:1), but when she brings forth it is not to the author of her visitation, but to him who seeks to win wisdom, whose name is Abraham" (II, 35).

Referring to his textual version of Genesis 18:12, in Sarah's saying "Not yet hath happiness befallen me till now but my Lord (the divine Word) is greater," he clearly identifies "Lord" with the divinity and not with Abraham, as the usual interpretation has it (I, 149–151; compare p. 116, above).

He interprets Genesis 18:11, in which it is said that "it ceased to happen to Sarah the manner of women," to indicate not, as the classical rabbinical interpretation has it, that Sarah ceased to be menstruous, but rather that she passed back from womanhood to virginity, in preparation for her union with God. "But among the virtues some are ever virgin, some pass from womanhood to virginity, as Sarah did: for it ceased to be with her after the manner of women (Gen. xviii, 11), at the time when she first conceives Isaac. . ." (II, 405). For Philo "the manner of women" is taken to mean the lack of virginity, and ceasing to have the manner of women is thus to have restored virginity.

According to Philo, Leah, Rebecca, and Zipporah were also made pregnant by God; and they then gave the products of these unions to their preferred lovers who sought their favor (II, 37).

Philo expresses misgivings about revealing such interpretations:

The virtues have their conception and their birth-pangs, but when I purpose to speak of them let them who corrupt religion into superstition close their ears and depart. For this is a divine mystery and its lesson is for the initiated who are worthy to receive the holiest secret. . . . The sacred revelation is not for those others who, under the spell of the deadly curse of vanity, have no other standards for measuring what is pure and holy but their barren words and phrases and their silly usages and ritual. (II, 35).

He beseeches his readers to keep his message secret: "These thoughts, ye initiated, whose ears are purified, receive into your souls as holy mysteries indeed and babble not of them to any of the profane" (II, 37).

OVID

I have been able to find another hint that some story of the divine conception of Isaac had wider circulation about the time that Philo lived. This is in the writing of Ovid, who lived some miles from Rome, and who was born 49 B.C. and died around 17 or 18 A.D. I believe that it is evident that the biblical story was the source of inspiration for Ovid's tale of the visitation of Jupiter and Mercury to the aged Hyrieus in *Fasti:*

Jupiter, and his brother who reigns in the deep sea, and Mercury, were journeying together. . . . An old man Hyrieus, who cultivated a tiny farm, chanced to see them as he stood before his little cottage; and thus he spoke: "Long is the way, but short the hours of daylight left, and my door is open to strangers." He enforced his words by a look, and again invited them. They accepted the offer and dissembled their divinity. They passed beneath the old man's roof, begrimed with black smoke; a little fire was glimmering in the log of yesterday. He knelt and blew up the flames with his breath, and drawing forth the stumps of torches he chopped them up. Two pipkins stood on the fire; the lesser contained beans, the other kitchen herbs; both boiled, each under the pressure of its lid. While he waited, he served out red wine with shaky hand. The god of the sea received the first cup. When he had drained it, "Now serve the drink," said he, "to Jupiter in order." At the word Jupiter the old man paled. When he recovered himself, he sacrificed the ox that ploughed his poor land, he roasted it in a great fire; and the wine which as a boy he had laid up in his early years, he brought forth stored in its smokey jar. And straightway they reclined on mattresses stuffed with river sedge and covered with linen, but lowly still. The table shone, now with the viands, now with the wine set down on it: the bowl was of red earthenware, the cups were beechen wood. Quoth Jupiter: "If thou hast any fancy, choose: all will be thine." The calm old man thus spoke: "I had a dear wife, whose love I won in the flower of early youth. Where is she now? you ask. The urn her ashes holds. To her I swore, and called you gods to witness, 'Thou shalt be my only spouse.' I gave my word, and I keep it. But a different wish is mine: I would be, not a husband, but a father." All the gods assented; all took their stand at the bullock's hide—I am ashamed to describe what followed—then they covered the reeking hide by throwing earth on it: when ten months had passed, a boy was born. Him Hyrieus called Urion on account of the mode of his begetting. The first letter of his name has lost its ancient sound."[29]

As in the story in Genesis 18, there is the extension of hospitality to strangers and the dissemblance of the strangers' divinity. The ox corresponds to the son-of-the-herd. The divine visitors recline as Hyrieus, like Abraham, has asked them (Genesis 18:4). Hyreius is equally concerned with the lack of offspring from his wife. He "would be, not a husband, but a father." The gods oblige by doing something regarded by the author as shameful at the bullock's hide. From this a child is born. The child is called "Urion on account of his mode of begetting," just as Isaac, whose name means coitus, gets his name from his mode of begetting.

At the time that Ovid wrote, there had been a connection between Rome and Palestine for a long time. Pompeius Trogus, a Roman contemporary of Ovid, wrote at some length of the history of the Jews in his *Universal History,* drawing in part from the Bible for his material. And Ovid himself was certainly sufficiently aware of the Jews to suggest in his *Ars Amatoria* that the Jewish Sabbath was a good day on which to begin a courtship. His exposure to at least some version of the biblical story is not unlikely.

SAMUEL, SAMSON, ELIJAH, ELISHA

The basic theme of Genesis 18 is repeated variously in the text, indicative of both the abiding character of that part of the saga and its significance. The repetitions also appear to have gone through a censorship process analogous to that associated with Genesis 18.

Consider the story of Samuel. A man by the name of Elkanah (I Samuel 1:11) has two wives, Hannah and Peninah, just as Abraham has Sarah and Hagar. Peninah, like Hagar, has children, but Hannah, like Sarah, does not. Elkanah prefers Hannah to Peninah. They go to the temple, where Hannah encounters Eli the priest at the door. She tells Eli what the cause of her unhappiness is, and he prays that she will have her petition granted. She vows that if she has a male child, that she will give him to YHWH.

Although Eli does not have a sexual role with respect to Hannah, that theme is subsequently presented in relation to Eli's sons, who "laid the women who served at the opening of the tent of the meeting" (I Samuel 2:22).

"And YHWH remembered her. And it was when the days were fulfilled and Hannah conceived and she bore a son and she called his name Samuel because from YHWH I asked for him" (I Samuel 1:19–20). This passage is parallel to "and YHWH visited Sarah as He had said, and YHWH did to Sarah as He had spoken. And Sarah conceived and bore Abraham a son to his old age at the time of which Elohim had spoken to him" (Genesis 21:1–2).

When Samuel is weaned, a bullock is sacrificed and the child is brought to Eli to serve in the Temple, reminiscent of the sacrifice of the ram instead of Isaac in Genesis 22.

In another tale (Judges 13) a certain Manoah has a barren wife. "And an angel of YHWH appeared to the woman and said, Behold now you are barren, and have not borne, but you will conceive and bear a son."

The woman recounts this visitation to her husband, and he prays that this "man of Elohim" should reappear. "And the angel of Elohim came again to the woman and she was sitting in the field; and Manoah her husband was not with her" (Judges 13:9). She runs and brings her husband. Her husband seeks to entertain the angel with food, as Abraham did. The angel refuses to eat, more consonant with the view that angels don't eat. The woman bears a son, and names him Samson.

Here we have again the barren wife; the appearance of a visitor, designated as both man and angel (Genesis 18:2 men; 19:1 angels), announcing the birth of a child; and the subsequent birth of the child. The child is to be a Nazarite, and no razor is to come near him, perhaps an allusion to the knife of Abraham that is not to touch

him. That Samson grows up to be a powerful fighter would appear
to tie this story to Genesis 6, which indicates that from such concep-
tions arise the Nephilim, the mighty men of fame (Genesis 6:4; see
pp. 23–24).

In yet another narrative Elijah, of Gilead, goes to Zarephath,
where he lives in the house of a widow during a drought. He meets
her at the gate of the city, and asks her to bring him bread in her
hand. The sexual suggestiveness of cakes has already been discussed
in connection with Sarah (see pp. 109 ff. above). The matter of a
woman baking and feeding cakes from the hand is also to be found
in the story of Amnon and Tamar (II Samuel 13:8).

She protests her poverty. He says "Do not be afraid. Go and do
as you have said. But make me a little cake from it first, and bring
it to me, and afterward make for you and your son" (I Kings 17:13).
He then tells her that the jar of meal and her cruse of oil will not
fail. He stays at her house for many days.

The widow's child gets sick. She says to Elijah: "What have I to
do with you man of God? Have you come to me to remind me of
my iniquity and to kill my son?" (v. 18). Jewish legend makes this
even more explicit with respect to Elijah's role. According to *Pirke
De Rabbi Eliezer* (in some of the manuscripts only), the reproach
of the woman of Zarephath is as follows: "Thou didst come unto
me for coition, and thou wilt bring my sin to remembrance against
me . . ." (p. 240).

Elijah carries the boy to his room upstairs and addresses God:
"YHWH, my God have you brought evil upon the widow with
whom I reside to slay her son?" (v. 20). He stretches himself on the
child, and the child revives. He brings the boy downstairs and says
to the woman, "See, your son lives."

The words spoken by the woman in this story indeed are an
allusion to the ritual associated with suspected infidelity described
in *Numbers:* "for it is a meal-offering of jealousy, a meal-offering
of memorial, a reminder of iniquity" (Numbers 5:15).[30]

Elijah becomes a divine figure who rescues children from death,
where perhaps that death is a punishment for the mother's deviation

from virtue. To this very day, in Jewish tradition Elijah is a regular visitor at the Passover service and a participant in every circumcision ceremony, in both of which jeopardy to children is involved. Indeed, Elijah is even referred to in the New Testament, where he is expected to come and rescue Jesus from death on the cross (Mark 15:35; Matthew 27:47).

In tradition Elijah is also the one who characteristically reconciles fathers and children: "Here, I send Elijah the prophet to you, before the coming of the great and the tearful day of YHWH. And he will turn the heart of fathers to the sons, and the heart of sons to their fathers, lest I come and strike the earth with a curse" (Malachi 3:23–27).[31]

Elisha, who was made a prophet by Elijah's casting his mantle over him (I Kings 19:19), frequently eats bread in the house of a woman of Shunem, "a great woman" (II Kings 4:8). She asks her husband that they furnish an upstairs room for his use.

One day when Elisha is in his upstairs room, he has his servant, Gehazi, summon the Shunemite woman. Through the servant, Elisha asks what he can do for her in appreciation for the care she has given. "Would you have one speak on your account to the king, or to the captain of the host?" he asks. She evidently declines, saying "I sit within my own people" (v. 13).

Elisha asks "What can be done for her?" and Gehazi answers: "But rather she has no son and her husband is old," suggestive of the Sarah and Abraham story.

So Elisha says, "Call her." Gehazi calls her and "she stood at the door," reminiscent of Sarah at the tent door. He says "At this time, at the lifing time you will embrace a son" (v. 16) the message from Genesis 18:14.

She replies, "Let not my lord man of God mislead your handmaid." "And the woman conceived and she bore a son at this time, at the lifing time as Elisha had said to her" (v. 17).

At a time when Elisha is gone from the house, the child dies. She puts him in the bed of Elisha and rides to find Elisha at Mount Carmel. She catches hold of his feet and says, "Did I ask a son of my lord? Didn't I say 'Don't mislead me?' " (v. 28). Elisha returns to the house and stretches himself upon the dead child lying in his bed, and the child returns to life.

Legend adds of Elisha that "no woman was able to gaze at his face without dying."[32] Legend also displaces the suggested sexual activity onto Gehazi, Elisha's servant. Gehazi, who has been singled out as one of seven who can have no share in the world to come (BT, Nezikin: Sanhedrin 90a), touched the genitals and breasts of the Shunemite woman.[33]

GABRIEL AND ELIZABETH, GABRIEL AND MARY

Zacharias, a priest, and his wife Elizabeth have no children, "because Elizabeth was barren, and both were advanced in years" (Luke 1:7). An angel appears to Zacharias, saying that "your wife Elizabeth will bear you a son, and you shall call his name John" (v. 13); that John would become "great before the Lord" (v. 15); and that John will be possessed of the "spirit and power of Elijah" (v. 17).

Zacharias says, "How shall I know this? For I am an old man, and my wife is advanced in years" (v. 18).

The angel tells him that he is Gabriel, who stands in the presence of God. Elizabeth conceives. She says, "Thus the Lord has done to me in the days when he looked on me, to take away my reproach among men" (v. 25).

The story is reminiscent of Abraham and Sarah. As in the case of Abraham, the angel appears to Zacharias. The promise that "your wife Elizabeth will bear you a son, and you shall call his name John" is virtually verbatim "but Sarah your wife will bear you a son, and you shall call his name Isaac" (Genesis 17:19). Zacharias's challenge is an allusion to Abraham's "to a son of a hundred years shall a child be born? Or shall Sarah, a daughter of ninety years, bear?" (Genesis 17:17).

The author's choice of Gabriel recalls that in the story of the visitation to Abraham the visitors are called "men" at one point (Genesis 18:2), and "angels" at another (19:1). In the Book of

Daniel, when Gabriel appears to Daniel, the text refers to him as "the man Gabriel" (Daniel 9:21). Thus for the author of the Book of Luke, an angel appearing in the guise of a man who is to perform an act like that of the men-angels in the Genesis story is aptly named Gabriel.

In the sixth month of Elizabeth's pregnancy Gabriel is sent by God to Mary in Galilee, a virgin espoused to Joseph:

> And he came to [in unto (King James)] her and said, "Hail, O favored one, the Lord is with you! [blessed art thou among women (KJ)]." But she was greatly troubled at this saying, and considered in her mind what sort of greeting this might be. And the angel said to her, "Do not be afraid, Mary, for you have found favor with God. And behold, you will conceive in your womb and bear a son, and you shall call his name Jesus." (Luke 1:28–31)

Mary asks, "How can this be, since I have no husband [seeing I know not a man (KJ)]?" (v. 34). The angel answers, "The Holy Spirit will come upon you, and the power of the Most High will overshadow you; therefore the chiid to be born will be called holy (therefore also that holy thing which shall be born of thee shall be called (KJ)], the Son of God" (vs. 34–35).

He tells her that her cousin Elizabeth has also conceived and is in her sixth month, "For with God nothing nothing will be impossible" (v. 37).

Mary says to him, "Behold the handmaid of the Lord; be it unto me according to thy word" (v. 38).

That the angel has sexual intercourse with Mary is quite unambiguous in The King James translation of Luke: "And the angel came in unto her." The words used in the Greek of Luke are the same as occur, for example, in The Septuagint to describe Judah's having sexual intercourse with Tamar, when she pretends that she is a prostitute. Judah gives Tamar his signet and cord as a pledge for later payment. The text says, "And he gave them to her, and came in unto her, and she conceived by him" (Genesis 38:18).

The words "For with God nothing is impossible" (v. 37) clearly alludes to "Is anything too difficult for YHWH?" (Genesis 18:14).

"Son of God" ties the story back to Genesis 6:1–4, both by the words "Son of God" and by theme.

The author of Luke has divided the basic elements from the Abraham-Sarah story and distributed them between the stories of Elizabeth and Mary. However, the allusion to the story of Genesis 18 is barely concealed by the simplistic device of spreading the thematic elements among two consecutive and related stories.

What is thereby achieved is a new beginning of the old saga, a "new covenant", starting all over again with a repetition of the story of Abraham, represented by Zacharias; and Sarah, represented by Mary; and the birth of Isaac, represented by the birth of Jesus. Yet there are major differences. Whereas Isaac is spared (Genesis 22), Jesus is not. Where Isaac has offspring, Jesus does not.

The story of Jesus rounded out the saga. It completed the story that had been essentially unfinished for about a millenium; as though Abraham's knife had been held suspended in the air over Isaac, the Son of God, for a thousand years. Always there was the question, as was so poignantly repeated over and over again in the writings of the prophets, of whether God would come and rescue his own Isaac. Would Elijah come and rescue Jesus from the cross (Matthew 27:47–49; Mark 15:35–36)? In the end there is no usual rescue; there is the resurrection. The story ends. In the ideology of the new Christianity Jesus alone becomes the Son of God, and God's "only [begotten (King James)] Son" (I John 4:9). The great diaspora of the Jews grew following the destruction of Jerusalem in 70 A.D. And Christianity began its great growth with Paul and his followers at about the same time.

NOTES

1. Compare Judges 19:24 and Exodus 21:10 for similar use of the word I have here translated as *cohabitation*. I am aware of the unusualness of this translation. The whole verse might be rendered: "Behold I have purified you, but not as silver. I chose you the first born of my cohabitation."
2. Gerhard Von Rad, *Genesis: A Commentary,* tr. John H. Marks (Philadelphia: Westminster Press, 1959), p. 110.

3. Cuthbert Aikman Simpson, *The Early Traditions of Israel* (Oxford: Basil Blackwell, 1948), p. 62.

4. See Simpson, pp. 62, 333; and translations. YaDuR occurs in some manuscripts. It is related to the word for generation, DOR.

5. *Pirke De Rabbi Eliezer,* tr. Gerald Friedlander (New York: Benjamin Blom, 1971), p. 160.

6. Simpson, p. 76.

7. *Aboth deRabbi Nathan* 30b, as translated in Lieberman, *Hellenism in Jewish Palestine* (New York: The Jewish Theological Seminary, 1962), p. 44.

8. Von Rad, p. 163.

9. *Niddah* is a menstruous woman. According to Jewish law, a Niddah is forbidden to have sexual relations with her husband. Various types of contact with a Niddah have been allowed and forbidden throughout history, and the topic is dealt with at great length in Jewish literature. Maimonides later maintained that the restriction on cooking from the hand of a Niddah as unclean—the point Rashi is making here—was devoid of significance.

10. John M. Allegro, *The Sacred Mushroom and the Cross* (New York: Doubleday, 1970), pp. 20–21.

11. Vance Packard, *The Hidden Persuaders* (New York: David McKay, 1957), p. 77.

12. See L. Levy, "Sexualsymbolik in der biblischen Paradiesgeschichte," *Imago,* V (1917–19), pp. 16–30.

13. David Bakan, *On Method* (San Francisco: Jossey-Bass, 1967).

14. Von Rad, p. 202.

15. There are some exceptions, such as in questions concerning the purity of women (BT, Nashim: Ketubbot 72a). This feature of rabbinic law was abolished in Israel by the Equality of Women's Rights Act of 1951.

16. Ginzberg, V, p. 237.

17. Leo Strauss, *Persecution and the Art of Writing* (Gencoe, Ill.: Free Press, 1952), p. 30.

18. J. Weingreen, *A Practical Grammar for Classical Hebrew,* 2nd ed. (Oxford: Clarendon Press, 1959), pp. 66–67.

19. Francis Brown, S. R. Driver, and Charles A. Briggs, *A Hebrew and English Lexicon of the Old Testament* (Oxford: Clarendon Press, 1975), pp. 115, 116.

20. In Genesis alone BLTY is pointed as BiLTiY in 3:11, 4:15, 19:21, 21:26, 38:9, 43:3, 5, and 47:18.

21. Henry B. Swete, *An Introduction to the Old Testament in Greek* (New York: KTAV Publishing House), 1968, p. 374.

22. VI Philo, tr. F. H. Colson and G. H. Whitaker (Cambridge, Mass.: Harvard University Press, 1958), pp. 56–61. Hereinafter referred to by volume number.

23. This translation is agreed to by Bowker, p. 212.

24. John Bowker, *The Targums and Rabbinic Literature* (London: Cambridge University Press, 1969), p. 208.

25. Simpson, p. 332.

26. *Philo Supplement. I. Questions and Answers on Genesis,* tr. Ralph Marcus (Cambridge, Mass.: Harvard University Press, 1953), p. 286.

27. Von Rad, p. 202.

28. Samuel Sandmel, *Philo's Place in Judaism* (New York: KTAV Publishing House, 1971), p. 174.
29. Ovid, *Fasti,* tr. J. G. Frazer (Cambridge Mass.: Harvard University Press, 1959), pp. 297–301.
30. The word here which is usually translated as iniquity is, indeed, the same word that I have said means coitus or cohabitation. See Chapter 8, note 1.
31. Malachi is divided into three chapters in the Masoretic text, but into four in the Septuagint and some English versions. Chapter 3, verses 19–24 of the Masoretic text is counted as Chapter 4, verses 1–6 in the latter. Thus this quotation is Malachi 4:5–6 in the RSV.
32. *Pirke De Rabbi Eliezer,* p. 241.
33. *Pirke De Rabbi Eliezer,* p. 241.

CHAPTER 9

The Affirmation of
Patrilineality

In this chapter I will attempt to indicate some of the features of the text that are relevant to the establishment of a patrilineal and patriarchal ideology.

THE BINDING OF ISAAC

The story that is recounted in Genesis 22:1–19, which describes how God commanded Abraham to sacrifice Isaac, the bearer of the promise that God had made to him, and called the *Akedah,* the binding, has played a leading role in the religious developments within Judaism, Christianity, and Islam. The Church fathers identified Isaac with Jesus. To this very day church altars are dedicated in the name of the altar on which Isaac was bound by Abraham. The Koran (Sura 37:99–115) alludes to the story of the binding. Islamic thought has sometimes replaced Isaac with Ishmael in the story. Numerous homiletic themes, such as those of faith, obedience, the superiority of animal to human sacrifice, the nature of moral suffering, the relationship between law and God's ultimate will, and the significance of martyrdom—to name only a few—have centered around this episode in the Bible. One of the great works of Kierkegaard, *Fear and Trembling,* considers Abraham's and Isaac's existential positions at the Akedah in detail.

The Akedah may also be seen as critical in the shift from matrilineality to patrilineality. It is ascribed to the E author. Since E comes from a period several hundred years later than J and several hundred years before P, E is historically transitional between the other two major documents, if we allow the documentary hypothesis. In the Akedah story E is also thematically transitionary between J and P with respect to matrilineality and patrilineality.

Elohim calls to Abraham in Genesis 22 and tells him, "Take now your son, your only one, whom you love, Isaac, and walk yourself to the land of Moriah, and offer him there as a burnt offering on one of the mountains which I shall tell you" (v. 2). Abraham takes Isaac, two young men, and wood for the burnt offering.

When they arrive in sight of the place, Abraham "took the wood of the burnt-offering and placed it on Isaac his son and he took in his hand the fire and the knife, and the two of them walked together" (v. 6).

On the way Isaac asks, "Here is the fire and the wood and where is the lamb for the burnt-offering?"

Abraham replies, "Elohim himself will show the lamb for the burnt-offering, my son" (v. 8).

Abraham builds an altar and binds Isaac on it. He stretches out his hand with the knife to sacrifice Isaac. At that point, an angel of YHWH calls out and tells Abraham not to lay his hand on the boy and not to cause him any injury, "for now I know that you are an Elohim-fearing man and you have not withheld your son, your only one, from Me" (v. 12). A ram appears in the thicket, and Abraham sacrifices the ram instead. Abraham calls the place YHWH-will-see.

One of the classic interpretations of this narrative is that it represents the great faith of Abraham, who would obey God even though in so doing he would destroy the basis of God's promise to him. The New Testament indicates, "By faith Abraham, when he was tested, offered up Isaac, and he who had received the promises was ready to offer up his only [begotten (KJ)] son, of whom it was said, 'through Isaac shall your descendants be named' " (Hebrews 11:17–18). I cite this only to indicate how deeply problematic this passage is, as it produces either error or distortion even in the author's perception of Genesis 22. For certainly the author knew that Isaac was not Abraham's only begotten son, since he had had Ishmael first.

I would like to suggest an addition to (not a denial of) the classical interpretation.

We note that the text contains the words "walk yourself" (LeCH LeCHa). These are the same as the first words of God addressed to Abraham telling him to leave his father's house (Genesis 12:1). I suggest that these are signal words in connection with patrilineality, overcoming matrilocality by mobility.

The naming of the place *YHWH-will-see* is parallel to the naming of place in the story where God rescues Ishmael from a death promoted by Sarah. The text says of the pregnant Hagar, "And she called the name of YHWH who spoke to her, 'You are a god of seeing,' For she said: Have I even here seen Him after my seeing? Therefore the well was called Well-to-life[1]-seeing" (16:13–14). This similar naming of place may indicate some editorial suggestion that the parental prerogative to kill a child has passed from female to male, essentially ascribing to the male what may have been a female prerogative, to Abraham what had been Sarah's prerogative over the child of her handmaiden. The combination of covenant, near-death, and rescue in the Abraham-Isaac narrative is parallel to the combination of covenant, near-death, and rescue in the Hagar-Ishmael narrative.

Most importantly, the text clearly reassigns *Sarah's parenthood* to Abraham in the words, "Take now your son, your only one, whom you love, Isaac." Abraham has two biologically begotten sons, Isaac and Ishmael. Isaac is the only biological son of Sarah not of Abraham. Rashi cites a beautiful hypothetical conversation from the Talmud (BT, Nezikin: Sanhedrin 89b) about this confusion:

> He said to Him, "Two sons have I."
> He said to him, "Your only one."
> He said to Him, "This is an only one to his mother, and this one is an only one to his mother."
> He said to him, "Whom you love."
> He said to Him: "I love both."
> He said to him: "Isaac!"

The problem is how Isaac can be "only" when Abraham is also the father of Ishmael. The text here seeks, in a sense, to meld the figure of Abraham with the figure of Sarah. It would have been appropriate for God to address Sarah with the speech, "Take now your son, your only one, whom you love, Isaac." By taking a speech that is appropriately addressed to Sarah as an address to Abraham, the text transfers the "motherhood" to the father.

This reassignment of parental role from the mother to the father is perhaps the most important part of this story. There is no indication that Abraham either consulted with Sarah or informed Sarah of his intention to sacrifice Isaac. Indeed, legend has it that Sarah died as a result of being told by Satan of Abraham's doings with respect to Isaac.[2]

A peculiarity with respect to the animals mentioned in the passage is to be noted. Whereas the conversation between Abraham and Isaac alludes to a lamb, a ram appears in the thicket. Elizabeth Gould Davis has argued that historically "the ram became a symbol of patriarchy.[3] If we allow this any validity, then the change from lamb to ram in the story may be symbolic of the shift to patriarchy.

Legend indicates that the rescuing angel who stops Abraham from killing Isaac is the same one who appeared to Sarah to tell her of the birth of her son. The angel is Michael. It is of interest that it is precisely Michael who is referred to in the Mass (Confiteor) after the mention of "Mary, ever Virgin," again suggestive of a Mary-Sarah parallel.

The theme of the rescuing God-father, who saves his own, has of course played a most significant role in both the Jewish and the Christian traditions, including the anguished cry of Jesus, "My God, my God, why hast thou forsaken me?" (Mark 15:34) and the people's expectation that the God-father Elijah would save him (Mark 15:35–36). The theme of God taking care of his own children, which is introduced in this manner in the Akedah, is critical to the subsequent development of the saga. For one of the essential features of the whole story is that Israel is God's people and that therefore he would then save them from their enemies, an expectation addressed by the prophets.

But in what sense is Israel God's people? In Exodus 4:22 we find

God saying to Pharaoh, "Israel is my son, my first born." In Isaiah, "I chose you as the first born of my cohabitation" (Isaiah 48:10; see also Chapter 8, note 1). In Psalms, "He said to me, 'You are my son. I today childed you'" (Psalms 2:7).

There was a general suppression of the theme of divine impregnation. However, the implication that God will do what he has to do to protect his own children from harm had an abiding value for the Israelites; and thus the concept of divine descent could not be completely eradicated.

The idea of God as father may well have been understood historically as more literal than metaphorical. Indeed, the profound crisis that occurred in the emergence of Christianity may perhaps be understood in terms of this issue. I believe that the deep significance of the notion of Jesus as the only begotten son is likely to be the reaction against the notion of the Jews as a whole having been begotten of God. The often-repeated verse, "For God so loved the world, that he gave his only begotten Son . . ." (John 3:16)[4] may be understood as part of the ideological spreading of the Christian idea to non-Jews. For, instead of the Jews at large having been begotten of God, now only Jesus was thus begotten. And, as I John has it, "that God sent his only begotten Son into the world, that we might live through him" (I John 4:9)[5] and "whosoever believeth that Jesus is the Christ is born of God" (I John 5:1). The New Testament several times cites the critical verse from Psalms 2:7 (Acts 13:33; Hebrews 1:5; Hebrews 5:5). Christianity thus made it possible for all who may not have had divine descent to participate in it nonetheless by transferring the divine descent to Jesus, in whom all believers could participate.

CONTRIBUTION OF P

The most powerful textual establishment of patrilineality is in the contribution of P and its secondary elaborators. P comes from the fifth, or possibly the sixth, century B.C. The P document is clearly a product of the exile, and is "directed towards serving as a legal foundation for the ardently longed-for reconstruction of people and religious community."[6] The P document is characterized by an emphasis on history, particularly genealogical history, precise dating of events, and law. P is much concerned with the circumcision, having contributed the seventeenth chapter of Genesis, in which the circumcision is established as the sign of the Covenant.

P contributes the genealogies. P is responsible for a "These are the generations of . . ." and the various "begats," as the Hebrew YaLaD has often been translated. It would, perhaps, be more accurate to translate these by allowing "child" to be a transitive verb as it is in Hebrew. Thus we would more accurately have "these are the childings of," instead of "these are the generations of"; and, for example, "And Noah childed three sons" (Genesis 6:10). The P document has the genealogies coming from Adam (Genesis 5:1), Noah (Genesis 6:9), the sons of Noah (10:1), Shem (11:10), Terah (11:27), Ishmael (25:12), Isaac (25:19), Esau (36:1, 9), Jacob (37:2), and Aaron (Numbers 3:1). In each of these verses only males are cited as progenitors.

It is interesting to note that whereas in the J story of creation man is first created and woman subsequently from the man's rib (Genesis 2:7), in the P version both sexes are made simultaneously, "male and female created he them" (Genesis 1:27).

It may be of value to cite some of the words characteristic of the P document,[7] for the words are indicative of the major concerns of the author(s):

Lineage: *tribe; throughout your generations.*

Ownership and inheritage: *be possessed, get possessions, have possessions, take possession;*[8] *possession; inherit, have inheritance, take inheritance.*

God speaking through another: *speak unto the children of Israel; and Jehovah spoke unto . . . saying.*

Commandment and trespass: *according to the ability, the command, the word of; at the commandment, the mouth of; by the command of; commit a trespass, trespass, trespass a trespass.*

Rebellion: *murmur, murmuring; rebel.*

People as a collective: *assemble selves, be assembled, gather selves together; congregation.*

Tabernacle: *tabernacle of Jehovah; service (or work) of the tabernacle.*

Priesthood: *be priest, minister in priest's office; priesthood.*

Sanctification: *hallow, sanctify.*

The P document is an intense effort to firm up patrilineal descent and the concomitant social and political organization. Patrilineal descent is strongly associated with the ownership of property. There is great emphasis on obedience. The direct communication with God that characterizes the J and E documents is virtually gone. P is very much concerned with the collective peoplehood in contrast to the individualistic thrust evident in the other writers.

THE CIRCUMCISION

The circumcision played a profoundly significant role in the establishment of patrilineality. It is a symbol in which several important meanings converge.

The great religious significance of the circumcision is largely associated with passages identified as being of the P document and is thus postexilic. We may note the difference between the covenantal passage in Genesis 15, which is a conflation of J and E, and Genesis 17, which comes from P. In Chapter 15 YHWH makes a covenant with Abraham in a ceremony involving the sacrifice of animals. In Genesis 17, however, which repeats the covenant with Abraham, there is no mention of animals; the covenant is solemnized by the circumcision. One may think of a development through Genesis 22:7–19, the Akedah, to the covenantal Genesis 15 entailing animal sacrifice, to Genesis 17, a covenant entailing circumcision. In Chapter 17 God says to Abraham:

> This is My covenant which you shall keep, between Me and you, and between your seed after you; circumcise among yourselves every male. And you shall circumcise the flesh of your foreskin; and it will be a sign of covenant between Me and you. And a son of eight days circumcise

among yourselves every male throughout your generations, he that is born in the house, and bought with money of any foreigner that is not of your seed. You must circumcise those born in your house and bought with money and it will be my covenant in your flesh as an eternal covenant. The uncircumcised male who does not circumcise the flesh of his foreskin, his soul will be cut off from his people; he broke My covenant. (Genesis 17:10–14)

The circumcision may be understood as representing God's having delegated his procreative prerogative to man. If, as I have suggested, the background context is one in which the idea of divine impregnation prevailed, the covenant constitutes a transfer of this prerogative with, as it were, God's mark, the mark of the covenant, upon the penis. The saga indicates that the transfer was made from God to the patriarchs. God is presented as relentlessly nonsexual, whereas human males are clearly generative. The transfer of this sexual-generative license is then passed along from father to son throughout the generations. As has been indicated previously, the circumcision is characteristically associated in the text with a blessing for fertility. With this transfer of prerogative, the remainder of the text would seek to remove indications of divine impregnation, except in some of the traces which we have identified.

This mark, transferred from father to son, also represents title to land. I suggest that the authors of the P document were reacting to the exile, and its threat to title to land as well as to identity. We recall that the earlier exile of the North had resulted in dissolution of the people, and the authors of the P document did not want that to occur again; they were interested in establishing, or certainly perpetuating, a mark of permanent title to the land that could be transgenerational. The practice of circumcision would allow the transfer of title patrilineally through the generations indefinitely. The circumcision, called the BRiT, the covenant, is, according to the text, linked to the inheritance of the land of Canaan (Genesis 17:8).

With the circumcision the male is, in some senses, converted into a female. In the circumcision ceremony the father essentially claims and recognizes the child as his own, and binds himself to provide

maintenance, protection, and education for the child. In the ceremony the child is given a name by his father, even as it is recorded in
the New Testament (Luke 1:59), although circumcision was
dropped by the early Christians (Romans 3:4; Acts 5:15). In classical
form the circumcision entailed the *mezizah,* in which the father
drank the blood of the son. In this way the blood bond was affirmed,
transcending all possible doubts about who the actual father of the
child might be. Elijah, the savior of children, is also presumed to be
present at the ceremony. In reciting the blessing, the father refers
to the commandment to introduce his son to "the covenant of
Abraham, our father," and as he is introduced into the covenant, "so
may he be introduced to Torah, the canopy of marriage, and good
deeds."

The circumcision has also been regarded as a token sacrifice of the
child, with the foreskin of the child sacrificed instead of the child's
life. Commentary has often identified the circumcision ceremony
with the almost-sacrifice of Isaac on Mt. Moriah.

The circumcision has been linked in tradition with two holidays,
the Passover and Yom Kippur. Abraham was supposed to have been
circumcised on the Day of Atonement, and therefore "Every year
the Holy One, blessed be He, sees the blood of our father Abraham's
circumcision, and He forgives all the sins of Israel."[9] Another tradition makes Passover the day on which Abraham was circumcised
(BT, Nezikin: Baba Mezia 86b). Tradition modified the story of the
Passover by adding the blood of the circumcision to the blood of the
lamb: "The Israelites took the blood of the covenant of circumcision, and they put it upon the lintel of their houses, and when the
Holy One, blessed be He, passed over to plague the Egyptians, He
saw the blood of the covenant of circumcision upon the lintel of
their houses and the blood of the Paschal lamb, He was filled with
compassion on Israel. . ." (*Pirke De Rabbi Eliezer,* p. 210; compare
Exodus 13:3 ff.).

The theme of effeminization of the male is remotely suggested
at one point in the text by having Abraham addressed in the feminine (Genesis 16:5). Vowels have been added to the consonantal text
so that it is vocalized as masculine. Rashi, however, takes pains to

indicate that it is, and should be, vocalized in the feminine: "between me and thee (fem.)." The possibility that female circumcision antedates male circumcision[10] also suggests that circumcision is associated with the effeminization of the male.

The story of sodomy (Genesis 19:1 ff.) that follows the visit of the angels to Abraham and Sarah may perhaps be interpreted as a authorial device to hint at some kind of relationship between God and Abraham in which males are, on the one hand, kept as males, while on the other hand, they may be sexually "known" as females. YHWH says of Abraham that he has "known him": "For I have known him, to the end that he may command his children and his houshold. . ." (Genesis 18:19). Shortly thereafter we find the Sodomite request, "bring them out into us, that we may know them" (Genesis 19:5).

A clear association of caretaking with the effeminization of the male can be seen in a complaint that Moses makes to God. Moses is described as deeply resentful of the burdens of caring for the people. Moses hears the weeping of the people when they are dissatisfied with manna and want other things to eat (Numbers 11:1–10). In response to hearing "the people weeping, family by family, every man at the door of his tent" (v. 10), Moses complains to God for having laid the burden of all the people on him. And then he says to God: "Have I conceived all of this people? Have I childed them that you should say to me, 'Carry them in your bosom, as a nurse carries the nursling' . . . ?" (11:12).

Thus we see here both the effeminization associated with being a father in the new tradition as well as an expression of resentment toward it. Moses accepts the concept, but he argues that they are not *his* children.

The by now classical psychoanalytic explanation of the circumcision is that it symbolizes and substitutes for the castration of the male.[11] If we accept this psychological explanation, it follows that the circumcision also represents a psychological effeminization. Another psychoanalytic interpretation comes from Frank Zimmerman, who observes that the circumcision is symbolic of fertility in a particular manner. He notes that in an uncircumcised male the glans of the penis is covered by the foreskin when the penis is not erect. When the penis is erect, the foreskin is retracted and the glans is exposed. A circumcised penis with the glans exposed is like a penis in the condition of erection and is therefore symbolic of sexual power and fertility:

> The intent of the circumcision becomes clear. A circumcised penis is a copy of a penis in erection. In other words, the ancient Hebrew unconsciously thought as follows, "May the penis of this infant now circumcised by always sexually potent and fertile, and ready to fertilize as if in a permanent erection." Circumcision in essence stems therefore from deep-seated anxiety,—the anxiety that one may be left without children; positively put: from the desire to insure the fertility and continuity of sons and sons' sons.[12]

If castration and fertility correspond to psychological reality, then the circumcision exhibits remarkable symbolic ingenuity. In the combination the male is made by circumcision into a *fertile castrate,* analogous to the normal female. It allows, as the text has it, El Shaday, the god of the breast (see p. 74 ff.) to address Abraham, "Walk before me, and you will be perfect" (Genesis 17:1). With the circumcision, the male is made into a procreator, as the female was previously understood.

Even men could be thought of as barren as a result of the covenant. For the text indicates that, in keeping the covenant, YHWH promises "You will be blessed among all the peoples; there will not be a barren male and barren female [among you]" (Deuteronomy 7:14). And men could be in a position of providing food appropriate for babies in "a land flowing with milk and honey" (Exodus 3:8). If the circumcision is not performed, and the male is not converted into a fertile castrate, then the consequence is that "that soul shall be cut off from his people" (17:14), which has characteristically been interpreted as being childless (Rashi, ad locum 17:14).

Circumcision is closely associated with the historical bar to intermarriage for the Jews. Although the main impact of the text is to promote patrilineality, nonetheless, there is a good deal of material that also speaks strongly to the appropriateness of matrilineality.

Indeed, as I have already indicated, the ultimate definition of an Israelite in the abiding Jewish tradition is to be out of a Jewish mother.

The issue of matrilineality versus patrilineality is important only where there is exogamy; under endogamy the issue simply does not arise. For if marriages take place only within the group, the lineages of the male and the female are in common, and a position on whether identity goes through the female or the male is not required.

The significance of the circumcision in maintaining endogamy is suggested by a verse in Isaiah (52:1): "For not anymore will the uncircumcised and the unclean come into you again." "Come into" characteristically means sexual intercourse. It is precisely the penis which is marked by the circumcision, and it is precisely a male who has issued from a Jewish female who is thus marked. If sexual intercourse is limited by women, allowing only circumcised penises to come into them, as Isaiah puts it, then one could talk about the children of the fathers in confidence that they are equally descended from the mothers. The circumcision provides evidence of appropriate descent of the male to an Israelite female about to have sexual intercourse. In the Pentateuch the prohibition against intermarriage specified seven peoples—the Hittite, Girgashite, Amorite, Canaanite, Perissite, Hivite, and Jebusite (Deuteronomy 7:1–4). Following the reforms of Ezra (Ezra 10:9 ff.), the prohibition was extended to all non-Jews. It is interesting, however, that with the major exception of Esther, the Bible hardly even entertains the notion of a Jewish female marrying a gentile male (see also I Chronicles 2:34).

The Dinah story is instructive in our understanding of the relationship between endogamy and the circumcision. The story comes from a considerably later hand even than P. According to Simpson, "The Dinah story was later added, probably in an attempt to provide a precedent in the light of which might be solved the problem of mixed marriages which continued to trouble the leaders of the post-exilic Palestinian community, even after the promulgation of the P code."[13]

In the story, the Prince of Shechem, son of Hamor the Hivite, has intercourse with Dinah. But he loves the girl and wants her to be his wife. He tells this to his father Hamor and asks his father to get him this girl as a wife. His father approaches Jacob with a proposal of marriage on his son's behalf. Dinah's brothers protest that they cannot give their sister in marriage to a man who is not circumcised. They say that they will allow the marriage only on the condition that every male Shechemite be circumcised. The Shechemites agree, and all are circumcised. However, when the Shechemites are lying in pain, Dinah's brothers Simeon and Levi go out and kill them all. "And they said, 'Should one deal with our sister as a harlot?'" (Genesis 34:31).

This story reveals a clear belief that, on the one hand, only a circumcised penis may enter into the body of an Israelite woman. On the other hand, it is also clear that the circumcision has to be *authentic*. Mere physical circumcision is not enough. But what does authentic mean? Only a male born of an Israelite woman can have an authentic circumcision, one that represents lineage. Thus while the circumcision became symbolic of patrilineality, it also ensured that not too much violence would be done to the ancient matrilineality.

The text also strongly suggests that only a child whose father was circumcised at the time of conception appropriately belongs to the Israelite community. Although Abraham has two sons and both are circumcised, Ishmael was conceived while Abraham was not yet circumcised, and Isaac was conceived after the circumcision of Abraham. Thus the Covenant applies to Isaac but not to Ishmael. A problem arises in connection with the twin sons of Isaac, Jacob and Esau. If they are twins, they arise out of a single instance of sexual intercourse. Then if Jacob is authentic in this sense, certainly Esau should be too. Jewish legend attempted to cope with the problem that, while Esau would have been circumcised, he was still not so closely tied to Isaac. One legend is that, although Isaac circumcised both Jacob and Esau, Esau despised the circumcision (*Pirke De Rabbi Eliezer*, p. 209). Another legend is that Jacob was born circumcised; and although Isaac circumcised Esau on the eighth day properly, Esau later subjected himself to an operation that made him look as though he had never been circumcised.[14]

Marriage, as a feature of the political and social context, potentially performs two contrary functions. On the one hand, it can be a method of absorbing other peoples and establishing political unification. At the same time, it can be the method by which a people is absorbed into others and loses its identity. That both these possibilities are real may account for some of the text's ambivalence toward intermarriage of an Israelite male with a Gentile woman. Early in the history of the kingdom intermarriage could be used as a major device for absorbing large numbers of people and achieving political unity. This was clearly the use that Solomon made of marriage.

The story of Moses's taking a Cushite wife (Numbers 12:1 ff.) arises out of the period in which intermarriage was viewed relatively favorably. In this story, in which Moses is criticized by Aaron and Miriam, God is clearly supportive of Moses. However, an interesting feature of this story bears on the conflict between matrilineality and patrilineality. Although in the story both Aaron and Miriam would appear to be equally culpable in having criticized Moses, only Miriam is punished. God says, "If her father had spit in her face, should she not be shamed seven days? Let her be shut out of the camp seven days, and after that be brought in again" (Numbers 12:14). Moses's taking a Cushite wife asserts that patrilineality counts and matrilineality does not. Thus only Miriam, representing, as it were, the resistance of women to the reduction in their status, is punished. Moreover, as God's punishment of Miriam is in the order of a father spitting on a daughter's face, the story implicitly acknowledges a father's right to do this. Thus not only lineage, but authority as well, is ascribed to the male side. In other words, the text is seeking at this point to establish a *patriarchy* in addition to a *patrilineality*.

THE FIRST BORN

Probably one of the most awe-inspiring ideas we find in the Bible is that the first-born child belongs to God. That thought is repeated variously in the text. I suggest that the development of that idea is critical in the change from a matrilineal to a patrilineal social organization. One of the deep problems associated with the text is whether the first born of the male or the female is to be understood. Whereas BeCHOR, first born, is sometimes identified clearly with the female, as PeTeR ReCHeM, the opener of the womb (Exodus 13:1), it is also identified with the male, as in the address of Jacob: "Reuben, you are my B'CHOr, my strength and the ReiSHiYT oNiY"— my first born, the first of my cohabitation (Genesis 49:3). The rabbinical tradition distinguished first born matrilineally by virtue of the opening of the womb and patrilineally by virtue of the first fruits of male cohabitation (BT, Kodashim: Bekoroth 47b). Inheritance was linked patrilineally on the grounds of Deuteronomy 21:15, which granted inheritance in the case of a man with two wives to the first born of the male, even though of the hated wife.

Ambivalence about the first born's belonging to God prevails throughout the text. The first born is to be killed, and the first born is subject to special protection. The first born has special status in terms of sanctification, and the first born is in distinct jeopardy until redeemed. The first born's death or near-death has a special place in the religious drama as exemplified in the stories of Jesus and Isaac.

There is substantial evidence that human sacrifice was prevalent in ancient Palestine at least until the seventh century B.C.[15] Julian Morgenstern has suggested that the killing of the first born was first an institution associated with matrilocal and matrilineal marriages, and that the actual killing of the first born was done by the brothers of the mother. Religiously, it was a concession to the prerogative of the gods arising from belief in divine impregnation. Socially, there existed ties of affection between the mother and her brothers that were threatened by the first offspring of the mother; thus the child was an appropriate sacrifice to the matrilineal deities. Morgenstern suggests that the odd fragment concerning circumcision in connection with Moses, Zipporah, and their child in Exodus 4:24–26 is explained on the basis of this ancient practice. By taking his wife and child away from their matrilocal location, Moses threatened the matrilineal Kenite clan deity, who was about to lose what was hers, the sacrifice of the first-born child. That deity therefore attacks the child and tries to take its life. Zipporah saves the child by promptly performing a circumcision to pacify the deity.[16] It is precisely in the transition to the new kind of marriage, patrilineal and patrilocal, that child sacrifice is stopped. The father assumes new protective responsibilities for the first born, whose death was symbolic of the matrilineal-matrilocal form of marriage to be overcome. Hence we find in the text the classical assertion of the first born belonging to God, but with additional provisions that would allow that the first born not be slaughtered. In rescuing the child from the female deity, the father overcomes her power.

The shift to animal sacrifice is critical in the establishment of patrilineality. It allowed the maintenance of the institution of sacrifice, but without the killing of human offspring. This meaning of sacrifice is quite different from the idea, developed by Freud in *Totem and Taboo,* that sacrifice is the killing of the father figure and the basis for unification of the brothers.

In the Book of Numbers we see a radical modification in the idea of the first born's belonging to God. YHWH instructs Moses: "Take the Levites instead of all the first born of the children of Israel and the animals of the Levites instead of their animals and the Levites will be mine; I am YHWH" (Numbers 3:45). And since the number of first born exceeded the number of the Levites, Moses is commanded to collect five shekels apiece for the excess to the priests (Numbers 3:45–48). The latter was the "redemption money" (Numbers 3:51).

By the time of Ezekiel a radically new view had developed—the fantastic theological notion that one of God's methods of punishing is to give bad commandments, and, in particular, the commandment to give the first born to God (Ezekiel 20:25–26; see also p. 53). The association of child sacrifice with the departure from righteousness is clear in Ezekiel, who was unenthusiastic about the idea that the first born belongs to God in the first place. Thus Ezekiel complains, "And you took your sons and your daughters, which you bore to Me, and sacrificd them to be eaten. Just a trifle of your whorings?" (Ezekiel 16:20).

MOBILITY

The traveling male who takes his family with him is basic to the social affirmation of patrilineality. The first words of YHWH addressing Abram are *LeCH LeCHa* (Genesis 12:1), translated in King James as "Get thee out." It may be translated, accepting the usual vocalization, as "Walk thyself." Rashi suggests "walk, for your own benefit and your own good." Or perhaps, since the consonantal form of the two words is identical and they can be read as *LeCH LeCH,* it might be simply, "Walk, walk." This commandment is addressed to a male head-of-household and clearly intends mobility of the whole household.

Paul Tillich once said that one of the important contributions of the Jews to civilization was the idea of a portable god. The gods of ancient times were characteristically place gods. The word *Baal,* which was often the first part of the name of a god, means master or lord. Thus, for example, Baal-hermon (I Chronicles 5:23) means the master, or lord, of Mt. Hermon. The specific location of the home of the Baal is characteristically referred to in the text as a high place. The worship of such place gods was ubiquitous in ancient Palestine and became the target of the believers in YHWH, who was associated with mobility.

The YHWH religion, as expounded in the text, indicates a patriarchal form of social organization that could be relatively independent of place. A major feature of the patriarchal saga is the mobile group that could maintain its identity on the basis of kinship rather than location. The largest part of the Pentateuch, recounting the lives of the patriarchs and the desert life of the Israelites, is of the wandering of the kinship group as a whole. Its social significance inheres, in large part, in its demonstration of complex and orderly social organization that could be sustained and perpetuated independent of place.

The text, we must remember, came into being in a context of relatively fixed location, coupled with an intense need to achieve unification and nationhood, a time of the establishment of federalism in the ancient land. The old forms of matrilineality and matrilocality, and the corresponding loyalties to the local gods, were inappropriate for the fashioning of larger economic, political, and especially military unification. Thus there was a shift to a divine being who was relatively independent of place yet located in one place—the temple conceived by David and built by Solomon, at the capital of the federation.

The story of the tower of Babel (Genesis 11:1-9) may help us understand the mentality behind the composition of the text. The aim that the text ascribes to the builders was to prevent dispersion of people by fixing a location marked by the high tower, "lest we be scattered on the face of all the earth" (Genesis 11:4). The authors interpret this aim as an affront to YHWH and ascribe to him a counteraction, the confounding of language, which results precisely in the people's being scattered "upon the face of all the earth" (11:9).

We can reasonably ask what "sin," as sins are generally understood in the remainder of the text, was committed by the builders of the tower. On the surface there appears to be no violation of any ethical principle. But the authors sensed in the proposed building project, aimed at reducing mobility, a gross inconsistency with the message expressed in the words LeCH LeCHa. For LeCH LeCHa, the first commandment to the first patriarch, is a mobility commandment. It overcomes the limited matrilineal and matrilocal forms of social organization. It is antithetical to the nature of YHWH, who is designed to be a god for people who are not tied to particular parcels of land.

The idea of such a non-landlocked god is important to the whole subsequent history. It certainly served the Jews of the diaspora in that their god went with them wherever they went. It was a significant feature in the acceptance of the text for later Christian empires. The image of the Son of God was, as sketched out in the New Testament, even more land-transcendent than YHWH, having no interest in the land at all. Indeed, the deep-lying ideology of federalism in the text may well have been a factor in the widespread acceptance of the text in subsequent history.

In the Bible the image of a traveler was someone whose mobility was with his kinship group. The contemporary fantasy of mobility is expressed in an unmarried, unattached cowboy type, a fantasy that also appeared in the Punch and Judy drama and the influential *Faust* of Goethe. These images are more conditioned by the mobility in the New Testament than by Abraham, Isaac, Jacob, or Moses.

PROPERTY: ZELOPHEHAD'S DAUGHTERS

The role that land played in entrenching patrilineality is evident in the story concerning Zelophehad's daughters.

Moses allocates the land on a patrilineal basis. However, Moses is presented with a complaint from the five daughters of Zelophehad, the grandson of Gilead. We have already indicated the marginal quality signaled by the biblical use of Gilead. Their father died in the wilderness, leaving no sons, and they plead, "Why should the name of our father be done away from among his family, just because he had no son? Give us a holding among the brothers of our father" (Numbers 27:4).

Moses takes their case to YHWH, and YHWH says:

> It is as the daughters of Zelophehad say. Surely give them a holding of inheritance among their father's brothers and hand over the inheritance of their father to them. And to the children of Israel say, saying, "should a man who has no son die, you shall hand over his inheritance to his daughter. And if he has no daughter, give his inheritance to his brothers. And if he has no brothers, give his inheritance to the brothers of his father. And if his father has no brothers give his inheritance to his kinsman that is next to him in his family, and he shall inherit it. And it will be a statute of judgment to the children of Israel as YHWH commanded Moses." (Numbers 27:7–11)

Thus the law of inheritance is in terms of male consanguinity, except that, when a man dies and leaves no son to inherit, women may inherit.

But the story does not end there. Presently the heads of the father's houses of the family of the children of Gilead come before

Moses and the leaders with a complaint against this decree of YHWH:

> YHWH commanded my lord to give the land for inheritance by lot to the children of Israel. And my lord was commanded by YHWH to give the inheritance of Zelophehad our brother to his daughters. But should they be wives to any of the sons of the tribes of the children of Israel, then their inheritance will be taken away from the inheritance of our fathers, and will be added to the inheritance of the tribe to which they will belong; and it will be taken from the lot of our inheritance. (Numbers 36:2–3)

Moses responds to this plea with a revision:

> It is so what the tribe of the sons of Joseph say, . . .As is good in their eyes let them be wives, except that they can be wives only in the family of the tribe of their father. So shall no inheritance of the children of Israel move from tribe to tribe; for everyone of the children of Israel will cling to the inheritance of the tribe of his fathers. (Numbers 36:5–7)

Accordingly, the daughters of Zelophehad marry their father's brothers' sons "and their inheritance remained in the family of their father" (vs. 11–12).

This text exemplifies the major problem that is introduced when kinship and inheritance converge, and the confounding that exogamous marriage may introduce. The historical problem is how an orderly pattern of inheritance can exist that would not destroy the integrity of the holding of land or, in connection with royalty, the integrity of the domain that is ruled. The problem of how to have unpartitioned inheritance without unfairness to all of the deserving heirs has been the subject of endless historical patterning and conflict. The total simplicity of matrilineality and matrilocality with respect to this issue is patent. However, with the introduction of mobility of women and families, and the increasing significance of military conquest for the possession of land, some criteria of discrimination among deserving heirs were necessary.

One criterion, which appears to have been well established in the thinking associated with the text, is that of the primacy of males over females, and for inheritance to be primarily from males to males.

The Zelophehad story illustrates a kind of embarrassment. An implicit first ruling is that all inheritance shall be through the male. Then arises the second ruling—in the event that a man has no sons, then his daughters can inherit, which appears to be fair. However, along come the complainers from Gilead with the very reasonable objection that such a decree would lead to violation of the integrity of land, with ownership passing to the tribes of whatever husbands the daughters of Zelophehad chose to take. Then the revised decree states that they can choose anyone they want, provided they choose husbands only from their own families. In other words, the ultimate solution is to develop a rule against exogamous marriages.

The patriarchal saga had already taken such an endogamous position in that, alongside the obvious male line of Abraham, Isaac, and Jacob-Israel, the four major "mothers" of Israel are also related to each other—Sarah, Rebekah, Leah, and Rachel all come from the same family. In a more general sense of extending the endogamous group from the limited family in the Zelophehad story to all the presumptive descendants of Jacob, the basic historical pattern of Jews since Ezra has been endogamous. Indeed, the deep importance of the traces of matrilineality in the text may be recognized for the history of the Jews, providing biblical support to the continuing matrilineality implicit in the manifest endogamy of the Jews. And, in particular, the circumcision is important in that it marks the males who are born from Jewish mothers, indicating their eligibility to become the husbands of Jewish women.

WARFARE

Warfare was a major factor in the establishment of patrilineality, patriarchy, and the winning of land. Warfare was principally the activity of the men at the time when mass armies were required.

There is a trace in the text of women's involvement in warfare. But that trace, the Song of Deborah, is generally recognized as one of the oldest documents to have been incorporated into the Bible, dating from about 1125 B.C., before the establishment of the kingdom by David. The song, which is included in Judges (5:2–31), is a military victory song associated with a woman. It describes the poor condition in the nation, when "the roads ceased, and the walkers on paths walked on the crooked roads. The rulers ceased in Israel. They ceased until Deborah arose, arose a mother in Israel." The song also describes how another woman, Jael, drove a tent pin with a hammer through the temples of Sisera, the escaped leader of the conquered enemy (Judges 5:24–37).

Thus ancient evidence implies a role for women in warfare. However, the idea of mother as a kind of military protector is extremely alien to the rest of the text. It was replaced by an alternative view of women as incapable of defending their right to water for their flocks but who could be protected by a single male (Exodus 2:16–17), who come out of the cities with song and dance to meet victorious troops (I Samuel 18:6–7), and so on.

The more normative relationship of sex and warfare in the period of the biblical composition is found largely in the Book of Numbers. The main source of Numbers is said to be P, and P's favorable attitude to the monarchy and the authority of chiefs and clan heads as archetypes of royal authority is evident in that book.[17] Here we have an account of the organization of the people of Israel into a massive fighting force. The male tribal names are essentially the names of regiments, and the families within the tribes are essentially the names of companies. Censuses are taken of warriors within each company and regiment. "Colonels" over the regiments and "captains" over the companies (to borrow modern military terminology) are named.

A military census is described at the beginning of the Book of Numbers. God tells Moses to "compute every head of all the congregation of the children of Israel according to their families, by their fathers' houses, according to the number of names, every male, by their polls, from twenty years old and older, all who can go out with the hosts in Israel, number them according to their hosts, you and Aaron. And with you there will be a man of each tribe, each a head of his father's house" (Numbers 1:2–4).

Such a military census is again repeated for the period after the years in the wilderness, together with a listing of the families that make up the tribes—from Reuben, 43,730 (25:7); from Simeon, 22,200; etc. (Numbers 26:1–51). The total is recorded as 601,730 (26:51), counted by males over twenty that "can go out with the hosts in Israel" (26:2). The Levites, important religiously but not militarily, are counted by the number of males from a month old and upward (26:62). There is a careful system of hierarchy with officers of thousands, captains of hundreds (31:48).

The land that they were to conquer is carefully designated (Numbers 34:3–12). The method of distribution of the land is designated in accordance with male warriors (Numbers 26:52–56). A system for distributing the spoils of warfare is established (31:25–54).

Several wars are indicated—wars with the Amelikites (Numbers 14), with the Canaanites (Numbers 14 and 21), with the Amorites (Numbers 21), with Balak (Numbers 21 and 22), and with the Midianites.

Military organization and discipline are clearly indicated. There is a fixed arrangement according to tribes in the camp (ch. 2). Trumpets are made and used as a way of giving signals (ch. 10). Insubordination, rebellion, and mutiny are dealt with by punishments (chs. 11, 12, 13, 14, 16, 17, and 21). Even Moses is punished for breaking discipline, as though to show that even the leader is subject to military discipline (20:7–13).

Chapter 14 is an oddity in the Genesis narrative. It places Abraham as a leader of a company of 318 trained male warriors in the midst of a war entailing great coalitions. From the documentary point of view it is very difficult to trace. It is not associated with J, E, or P. Von Rad says, "It is substantially, generically, and literally completely isolated and was apparently first incorporated into its present context by a redactor."[18]

However, it was evidently important to some compositor of the text that the founder of the whole tradition be clearly established as a warrior.

The organization of the people into a military force along patrilineal lines is not without objection even in the text. Let us recall that the story of Moses establishing this kind of military organization enters the text after such a military organization was historically established by David. Thus David's efforts at establishing a military organization undoubtedly conditioned the saga concerning Moses. But David's taking a census to organize the people into such a military establishment is clearly indicated as a sinful act, said to have been inspired by Satan! We find in I Chronicles: "And Satan stood up against Israel, and moved David to count Israel" (I Chronicles 21:1–2). The story continues with Joab exhorting David,

> "Why does my lord ask this [to be done]? Why should there be a guilt on Israel?" But the word of the King prevailed on Joab. And Joab went out and walked all over Israel and came to Jerusalem. And Joab gave the sum of the counting to David and there were in all Israel a thousand thousand and a hundred thousand men who could draw sword. And Judah four hundred and seventy thousand men that drew sword. But Levi and Benjamin he did not count because the King's word was an abomination to Joab. (I Chronicles 21:3–6)

The story continues of God's displeasure with David and the punishment. Most importantly, it recounts David's regret and his consequent decision to build the temple. Thus the very building of the temple is an act of restitution for the offense of conducting a military census.

The author of this story evidently takes it as given that David's effort at rationality in military preparation, using mathematics to determine the number of armed men that he might have available, is abominable. It is so abominable that Joab, even while carrying out his commander's orders, is at least partially disobedient in protest. What is the meaning of such antirationalistic, antibureaucratic sentiment within the biblical text? I believe that this is a major trace of resistance to the various social changes of the new federalism, introduced by David, which entailed a shift from matrilineal to patrilineal forms of organization. This federalism entailed a wrenching uprootedness from place, which had been associated with matrilineality; we can presume that all the moves associated with it were found odious and abominable. The meaning of David's response, to build a fixed rooted-in-place temple on the threshing floor of Ornan, thus becomes clear. He would give a place, a central place, for the new federation, analogous to the fixed places associated with the matrilineal clans.

When the saga of Moses, as told in the Book of Numbers, is composed, there is nothing abominable about taking a military census.

FEMALE RESPONSIBILITY

In the transition to patrilineality there is a major change in the nature of female responsibility. On the one hand, there is a significant increase in responsibility for sexual fidelity for women; on the other hand, there is a radical decline in female responsibility in other matters.

The ritual associated with female infidelity, from P, is designed to strike terror in the hearts of all women, however much it would appear to be tempered by justice:

> And YHWH spoke to Moses saying: Speak to the children of Israel, and say to them: If any man's wife should turn aside and do him an infidelity, and a man laid her a laying of seed and it be hidden from the eyes of her husband, secretly, and she defiled, and no witness against her, and she not exposed. And the spirit of jealousy come upon him, and he was jealous of his wife, and she was defiled; or if the spirit of jealousy come upon him, and he was jealous of his wife, and she was not defiled. Let the man bring his wife to the priest, and bring her offering for her, the tenth part of an ephah of barley meal; he shall not put oil on it, and not put frankincense on it. Because it is a meal-offering of jealousy, a meal-offering of memory, a memory of cohabitation. And the priest shall bring her near, and stand her before YHWH. And the priest shall take holy water in an earthen vessel and from the dust which is on the floor of the tabernacle the priest shall take and put it into the water. And the priest shall stand the woman before YHWH and unbind the woman's head and put on her hands the meal-offering of memory, which is the meal-offering of jealousy; and the priest shall have in his hands the waters of bitterness that curse. And the priest will swear her and say to the woman: "If a man did not lay you, and if you have not turned aside to defilement, while being under your husband, then be free from these waters of bitterness that curse. But if you have gone aside under your

husband, and if you are defiled, and some man has given you his laying other than your husband"—Then the priest shall swear the woman with the oath of cursing, and the priest shall say to the woman—"YHWH give you as a curse and a swearing among your people, when YHWH will make your thigh fall off and your belly swell; and these waters that curse will go into your bowels to make your belly to swell, and make your thigh to fall off" and the woman shall say "Amen, Amen." And the priest shall write these curses in a book and blot them with the waters of bitterness. And he shall make the woman drink the waters of bitterness that curse; and the waters that curse shall become bitter and will go into her. And the priest shall take the meal-offering of jealousy from the woman's hand, and wave the meal-offering before YHWH, and bring it to the altar. And the priest shall take a handful of the meal-offering, the memorial of it, and make it smoke on the altar, and afterward make the woman drink the water. And when he has made her drink the water, then it shall be, if she is defiled, and did her husband an infidelity, that the water that curses shall enter into her and become bitter, and her belly will swell, and her thigh will fall off, and the woman shall be a curse among her people. And if the woman is not defiled, and clean, then she shall be cleared and conceive seed. This is the law of jealousy, of a wife who is under her husband who goes aside and is defiled; or when the spirit of jealousy comes on a man, and he is jealous of his wife, then he shall stand the woman before YHWH, and the priest will do to her all of this law. And the man shall be clear from iniquity, and that woman will bear her iniquity. (Numbers 5:11–31)

The text distinguishes social responsibility for males and for females. "When a man vows a vow unto the Lord, or swears an oath to bind his soul with a bond, he is not to break his word; he shall do all that goes out of his mouth" (Numbers 30:3). However, if a woman takes a vow while she is in her father's house, then her father can void it (30:4–6). Indeed, the text patronizingly says that under these circumstances, "YHWH will forgive her, because her father disallowed her" (30:6). Similarly, if she is married, her husband can void her vow, and she is similarly forgiven (30:7–9). The text essentially keeps women subservient first to their fathers and then to their husbands: "These are the statutes, which YHWH commanded Moses, between a man and his wife, between a father and his daughter, while in her youth she is in her father's house" (30:17).

Our understanding of jealousy for infidelity in the minds of the composers of the text may be enriched by examining the brief passage associated with Lamech: "And Lamech said to his wives, 'Adah and Zillah, listen to my voice, wives of Lamech, hearken to what I say. For I have killed a man for wounding me, and a boy for bruising me. If the revenge of Cain is sevenfold, then for Lamech it is seventy-seven'" (Genesis 4:23–24). These two verses are regarded as additions after the narrative of which they are a part was composed.[19] These verses are placed immediately before "And Adam knew his wife again..." (Genesis 4:25).

In the apocryphal I Enoch, Lamech says of his son, "I have begotten a strange son, diverse from and unlike man, and resembling the sons of God of heaven; and his nature is different and he is not like us" (I Enoch 106:5). The author of I Enoch sees the motive of Lamech as a suspicion that the child that he has is the product of the union between one of his wives and the sons of God, as suggested by Genesis 6:1–4, which has been discussed earlier. Essentially the same thought is suggested in the Genesis Apocryphon of the Dead Sea Scrolls, which indicates that Lamech, who is the father of Noah (Genesis 5:28–30), accuses his wife: "Then I thought to myself that the conception was from the watchers and the holy one . . . and from the giants . . . and I was deeply troubled because of the child. So I went quickly to Beth-enosh [my] wife and said, 'Tell me [truthfully] and not falsely. . .'" (Genesis Apocryphon, Col. II).[20]

What meaning might be associated with the allusion to Cain in Lamech's song? Targum Pseudo-Jonathan indicates that Cain was equally the result of divine impregnation: "*And* Adam was aware that *Eve his wife* had *conceived* from Sammael the angel, and she became pregnant *and bare Cain,* and he was like those on high, not like those below; and she *said, 'I have acquired a man,* the angel of *the Lord'*" (Pseudo-Jonathan, Genesis IV:1).[21]

Pseudo-Philo, a piece of Hellenistic-Jewish literature, adds to Lamech's song: "I . . . have taken away sucklings from the breast."[22] The Book of Jasher, a thirteenth-century popular ethical book, has Lamech killing his son, Tubal-Cain, and "the wives of Lamech hated him from that day because he slew Cain and Tubal-Cain, and the wives of Lamech separated from him, and would not hearken to him in those days" (Jasher, II:33).[23]

Thus what has been included in the text may perhaps be a threat song by a male addressed to the female, a threat to kill the child which might be the product of an unfaithful union, a threat almost carried out by Abraham against Isaac. It is interesting to note that the rabbinical tradition attempted to temper this vaulting threat by Lamech. Rashi cites the Midrash as indicating that "Lamech did not kill anyone: but his wives separated from him when they had fulfilled [the commandment of] fruitful and multiply." Rashi also indicated that Lamech came to Adam to complain about his wives, and Adam told him, "Is it incumbent on you to be strict about the laws of the place? You do your duties and he [the ruler?] will do his."

THE IMAGERY OF FIDELITY

The story of Abraham and the Akedah provided an image of fidelity. In it Abraham acts as might the completely faithful wife asked by her husband, "How much do you love me? Do you love me so much that you would kill your child if I ask you to?" When Abraham responds positively, God essentially says, "You have proven your love for me. I do not want you to kill the child. Indeed, the child is mine too, and I will protect the child."

The Akedah story, combined with the material suggesting that God is the father of Isaac, serves to underscore two aspects of God: God as husband—to Abraham; and God as father—to Isaac. The image of God as both husband and father of the people of Israel prevails in the theological writing of the prophets. We see both of these ideas, for example, in two verses of Jeremiah. First, YHWH says, "How I remember you, the affection of your maidenliness, your love as a bride, how you followed me in the desert, in the unseeded land" (Jeremiah 2:1). This is immediately followed by "Holy is Israel to YHWH, his first produce. All who eat it will offend. Evil will come to them, declares YHWH" (Jeremiah 2:2). In the first verse, the people are a wife; in the second, produce.

The notion of God as husband and Israel as wife is very pronounced in Hosea. Hosea recounts his marriage to a specifically named woman, Gomer, who engaged in adultery. Hardly indicating any distinction between Gomer and the people of Israel, and ascribing the rhetoric of an outraged husband to God, Hosea discusses the defections of Israel.

Hosea also shifts between Israel as wife and Israel as child: "When Israel was a boy, and I loved him, and I called him out of Egypt as my son" (Hosea 11:1). He allows a "motherly" image of male child care: "And I taught Ephraim to walk, taking them by their arms. They did not know that I healed them. I drew them with red cords with weavings of love" (Hosea 11:3–4).

But with the Babylonian exile of the sixth century B.C. the increased need to firm up patrilineality made aspects of this image intolerable. Some break with the idea of divine impregnation and divine descent was essential. Ezekiel, even deviating from his contemporary Jeremiah, who was still influenced by Hosea, sought to do this by allowing God a role as husband to the people but not as their progenitor. In Ezekiel we find repeated over and over again the expression "Son of Man," a contrast to "Son of God," the latter being associated with divine descent, as in Genesis 6:1–4. In Ezekiel's imagery Israel is no longer the descendant of Sarah and Isaac in a land outside of Canaan. Rather, "Your origin and your childing are from the land of Canaan. Your father was the Amorite, and your mother a Hittite" (Ezekiel 16:3).

In Ezekiel's imagery Israel becomes an *adopted* daughter, a foundling cared for until she becomes nubile, at which time God marries her. God finds the cast-away infant in a field, unwashed and wallowing in blood. He takes her and cares for her. She grows up and becomes beautiful. Her breasts are fashioned, her hair is grown, and she comes into her time of love (Ezekiel 16:4–8). God spread his skirt over her and covered her nakedness. "I swore to you and I entered a covenant with you. A declaration of Adonai YHWH would you be to me" (Ezekiel 16:8). Thus Ezekiel allows the metaphor of God as husband. But the idea of Israel as descended from God is removed from the metaphor.

Ezekiel is otherwise very unenthusiastic about the significance of heredity. He openly rejects the commandment in which YHWH describes himself as a god who visits the iniquity of fathers on sons to the third and fourth generation (Exodus 20:4). For Ezekiel only "the soul that sins shall die. A son will not bear the iniquity of the father, and the father will not bear the iniquity of the son. The righteousness of one who is righteous will be on himself. And the wickedness of one who is wicked will be on himself" (Ezekiel 18:20).

Yet what remains of this imagery in Ezekiel is the notion that fidelity of people to God and the fidelity of a wife to her husband are essentially the same. The covenant of God and Israel is of the same order as the covenant extended to a woman in marriage.

NOTES

1. Or kinsfolk; see pp. 85–86.
2. Louis Ginzberg, *The Legends of the Jews,* Vol. I (Philadelphia: Jewish Publication Society, 1954), p. 278.
3. Elizabeth Gould Davis, *The First Sex* (Baltimore, Md.: Penguin Books, 1971), p. 134.
4. RSV deletes "begotten."
5. RSV deletes "begotten."
6. Otto Eissfeldt, *The Old Testament: An Introduction,* tr. Peter R. Ackroyd (New York: Harper & Row, 1966), p. 207.
7. Based on Cuthbert A. Simpson, *The Early Tradition of Israel* (Oxford: Basil Blackwell, 1948), pp. 410–414.
8. In the single instance in which this term occurs in the E document, Genesis 22:13, it has another meaning, *be caught.*
9. *Pirke De Rabbi Eliezer,* tr. Gerald Friedlander (New York: Benjamin Blom, 1971), p. 204.
10. *The New Encyclopaedia Britannica, Micropaedia,* 1977, volume II, p. 945.
11. Otto Rank, *Das Incestmotiv* (Leipzig and Vienna: Psychoanalytischer Verlag, 1926), p. 307; Theodor Reik, *The Temptation* (New York: George Braziller, 1961), p. 66.
12. Frank Zimmerman, "Origin and Significance of the Jewish Rite of Circumcision," *Psychoanalytic Review,* 1951, *38:* 103–112, 109–110.
13. Simpson, p. 121.
14. Robert Graves and Raphael Patai, *Hebrew Myths: The Book of Genesis* (New York: McGraw-Hill, 1964), pp. 189–190.
15. William Foxwell Albright, *Yahweh and the Gods of Canaan* (London: Athlone Press, 1968), pp. 207 ff.

16. Julian Morgenstern, "Additional notes on *Beena* Marriage (Matriarchat) in ancient Israel," *Zeitschrift für die Alttestamentische Wissenschaft* 1929, 49, 46–58, pp. 55–56

17. Y. Kaufmann, *The Religion of Israel,* tr. Moshe Greenberg (New York: Schocken Books, 1972), p. 185.

18. Gerhard Von Rad, *Genesis: A Commentary,* tr. John H. Marks (Philadelphia: Westminster Press, 1959), p. 170.

19. Simpson, p. 57.

20. Cited by John Bowker, *The Targums and Rabbinic Literature* (London: Cambridge University Press, 1969), p. 153.

21. Cited by Bowker, p. 132. The italicized words are in the Bible.

22. Bowker, p. 302.

23. *The Book of Jasher,* tr. M. M. Noah (New York: M. M. Noah and A. S. Gould), 1840.

CHAPTER 10

Conclusion

Throughout history symbols of both the classical matrilineality and patrilineality have existed in the traditional Jewish and Catholic marriage services. In traditional Judaism two features are essential to the service—the chuppah, which represents the ancient matrilineality and a covenantal declaration on the part of the groom: "Behold, you are holy to me, by this ring, according to the law of Moses and Israel." In the traditional Catholic service the matrilineal feature is maintained in that both the bride and groom take each other as husband and wife "according to the rite of our holy Mother, the Church"; and only the groom takes the vow, "to have and to hold, from this day forward, for better, for worse, for richer, for poorer, in sickness and in health, until death do us part." The Catholic service kept the Jewish asymmetrical ring giving and added a vow of *male* fidelity: "With this ring I thee wed, and I pledge thee my fidelity." Traditional Protestantism modified the Catholic service by having both the bride and the groom say "to love and to cherish" and "to have and to hold"; and kept the asymmetrical essential declaration from traditional Judaism in the form, "With this ring I thee wed: In the Name of the Father, and of the Son, and of the Holy Ghost," deleting the male's vow of fidelity of the Catholic tradition.

Where does this leave us? I began this essay by considering contemporary relationships, and I have pursued a path through some ancient history and detailed biblical exegesis. How may the exegesis bear on the contemporary situation?

I believe that two generalizations are of particular significance to the contemporary world. First, the Bible is associated with what is perhaps the most important step toward the reduction of male-female sex-role differences in the history of civilization. Second, the Bible is associated with the development of extended human organization for satisfying human needs.

SEX-ROLE DIMORPHISM

Two abiding facts concerning the human condition are significant to every form of human organization. The first is that women carry and give birth to babies, and men do not; the second is that the human infant and child require inordinate care after birth.

That women bear children and men do not is the ultimate basis for any male-female differentiation in sex roles in any society. There is no society in which there is no differentiation of roles on the basis of sex.

I believe that the foregoing exegesis clearly points to both a record of, and an ideology supportive of, a reduction of sex-role differences by the effeminization of the male, however paradoxical this may appear. That ideology acknowledged the role of males in the conception of the child, and it urged upon men a role in the care of the child after birth.

While the establishment of patrilineality brought with it certain of its own forms of sexual dimorphism, it reduced the difference between the sexes in obligation for care of the young.

The thought that men make a contribution to childing pervades the text. Men, by voluntarily engaging in coitus, conceive the child. By his abiding care for the child after birth, the male's role is authenticated. In the blush of the biological discovery, men tended to believe that the total genetic endowment was theirs. They were, of course, unaware of what we know today, of the halving of mitosis and the pairing of relatively equal halves in conception. They took the transitive verb, YaLaD, to child, as a word that could have a male subject. Psychologically they extended the boundary of the ego to include the sexual exudate and the offspring that resulted from it. They converted the despair associated with the recognition of personal mortality to the hope of indefinite biological existence through offspring.

Men allowed care of children to extend in various directions. By the conquest of land they provided milk, as in the "land of milk and honey." They extended care to entail major engineering projects, such as the building of a seaworthy ark in the face of an impending flood (Genesis 6:14 ff.), or a wall around Jerusalem, such as Nehemiah's. They rounded out the image of Abraham as a protective warrior. They made family the fundamental base for fashioning a mass army, the function of which would be the acquisition of land for themselves, women, and children. They based their enlargement of political bodies on the image of a male, Jacob, and his wives and concubines; and even larger political units on the basis of presumptive consanguinity through Ishmael, Lot, and Esau. By managing to overcome the hold of matrilocality, they provided a basis for family stability, even against the threat of dislocation from the land. The circumcision provided the ultimate claim to land and that could be maintained indefinitely.

One notion they could neither quite keep nor drop: the idea of divine impregnation. It was repressed, and yet it kept returning. On the one hand, God had to be deprived of procreative powers, with men claiming them and the claim authenticated in the circumcision. On the other hand, there was too much residual value in the idea of divine impregnation. It gave a concrete meaning to the idea of election. The idea of a male procreative God served to maintain the effeminization of the human male. It gave concrete meaning to the notion of fidelity to God, serving the metaphorical intentions of the prophets, as in Hosea. And ultimately it served the purpose of Christianity, which sought to transcend the particularity of the more limited kinship of the Israelites.

The fidelity of the male in providing for his offspring elicited the demand for sexual fidelity on the part of the female, guaranteeing that the offspring on whose behalf the male exerted himself were truly his. That image of female fidelity served as a model for the male's fidelity to God. Jealousy on the part of God was countenanced in parallel to a male's jealousy with respect to his wife. Though the male surrendered his masculinity in some senses, he was compensated in the form of license for jealousy.

Virginity of the female prior to marriage equally served to guarantee the paternal authenticity of the child. However, the lingering doubt concerning virginity prior to marriage played its role in the minds of the biblical authors, and was expressed in their profound ambivalence especially toward the child that "opened the womb" of the mother. From the larger social point of view virginity prior to marriage served to provide those children who were born with a male who was obligated to care for them.

By assuming major responsibility for the necessities of life for the household, the male also appropriated the authority to carry it out. As the guardian of the household, income producer, provider of education, and negotiator with the extrahousehold world, he claimed full accountability of members of the household to him. When he experienced his burden as great, he sometimes became moralistic, severe, and authoritarian, no different from the reaction of any contemporary overburdened parent or teacher, male or female. Not that this assumption of the "motherly" burden on the part of the male went unresented over history. Indeed, the enduring popularity in Western civilization of the Punch and Judy theme, in which Punch kills his wife and child and goes off to a life of complete debauchery, attests to this resentment. Moreover the male's demand for unqualified authority has been resented by the members of the household when it went beyond fulfilling the responsibilities.

Thus the sex-role dimorphism associated with the biblical patriarchal structure is based on the reduction of the dimorphism of men and women which in turn is based on the biological difference in connection with child rearing. It is of some interest in this regard that the traditional Jewish family, which we can presume to be under great influence of the biblical text, is characterized by extreme role flexibility of its members, with fathers easily assuming the maternal role toward the children and vice versa, and children easily assuming the role of parents to each other as well as toward their parents.[1]

As the demands of child bearing and rearing go down, so sex-role dimorphism goes down. Contraception, abortion, increased resources, reduction of the proportion of childing years of life span of the female—all serve to reduce sex-role dimorphism.

EXTENDED HUMAN ORGANIZATION

The history of the world may be divided into two major phases, dispersion and subsequent unification. At some point in the history of evolution human beings came into existence. Their numbers increased, and they dispersed. The dispersion paradigm is suggested in the Bible by the story of the Tower of Babel or the story of Abraham and Lot. In the latter the text indicates that "the land was not able to bear them that they might dwell together," leading to strife among them (Genesis 13:9). Abraham suggests to Lot: "Is not the whole land before you? Separate yourself, I pray you, from me; if the left, then I will go right; or if the right, then I will go left" (Genesis 13:9). The later history of the world is one of these diverse groups remeeting and recontacting each other, and the formation of ever more encompassing political and economic organizations. At this moment in world history we are virtually at the end of this second phase, with all people on the planet in contact with each other.

Our examination of the biblical text has indicated that the ideology of patrilineality played a significant role in this second phase. The kingdom was united under David and Solomon by the construction of the patrilineal kinship saga of Abraham, Isaac, and Jacob and their wives, Jacob being the most important. The prior matrilineal organizations were too restricted geographically to unify the people. And continued retention of matrilineality threatened to weaken the unity achieved, as the story of Zelophehad's daughters indicates.

Of particular significance was the increased need for military prowess and organization to provide protection. Although the story of Deborah provides an indication of female prowess in warfare, the superiority of men to women in fighting is suggested by such a story as that of Moses and the daughters of Reuel: "And the priest of Midian had seven daughters; and they came and drew water, and filled the troughs to water the flocks of their father. And the shepherds came and drove them away. And Moses rose and rescued them and watered their flock" (Exodus 2:16–17). The need for more reliable warriors entailed a shift to virtually completely male armies. The saga of organizing the people into a hierarchical military force along patrilineal lines is indicated in the book of Numbers. As has been suggested, that saga was undoubtedly conditioned by David's organization of the units along patrilineal lines.

It is to be noted that the idea of friendship, which is so commonplace today, hardly exists in most of the Old Testament. Friendship certainly is the central tie for Jesus and his disciples. And perhaps friendship was in the mind of the author of Job.[2] But the significant ties among people in the Old Testament are based on kinship. The only significant friendships in the earlier portions of the text are to be found in the story of Jonathan and David (I Samuel 18 ff.) and perhaps the story of Abraham and Melchizedek as recounted in Genesis 14, which was added to the main documents of the text later. Both of these friendships occur in a military context. I suggest that the prime locus for development of the very idea of friendship is situations calling for mutual protection in the face of enemies.

As the extension of human organization continued, the old idea of unity on the basis of descent from Jacob lost its value. Descent from God would serve better. I believe that the failure of the descent-from-Jacob saga to serve the larger unification process was one of the important bases for the development of Christianity. The notion of divine impregnation, which had been repressed during the formation of patrilineality, reemerged in the story of the birth of Jesus. For example, in his youth, Jesus responds to his mother's complaint about his absence, "Behold, your father and I have been looking for you anxiously," with "How is it that you sought me? Did you not know that I must be in my Father's house?" (Luke 2:48–49).

As the patrilineal saga had superseded matrilineality to extend unification, so did Christianity supersede patrilineality to extend unification further. The following passage may mark the precise instant of the birth of Christianity:

> And Jesus went away from there and withdrew to the district of Tyre and Sidon. And behold, a Canaanite woman from that region came out and cried, "Have mercy on me, O Lord, Son of David; my daughter is severely possessed by a demon." But he did not answer her a word. And his disciples came and begged him, saying, "Send her away, for she is crying after us." He answered, "I was sent only to the lost sheep of the house of Israel." But she came and knelt before him, saying, "Lord, help me." And he answered, "It is not fair to take the children's bread, and throw it to the dogs." She said, "Yes, Lord, yet even the dogs eat the crumbs that fall from their master's table." Then Jesus answered her, "O woman, great is your faith! Be it done for you as you desire." And her daughter was healed instantly. (Matthew 15:21–28; see also Mark 7:24–30)

Jesus first refuses to heal the daughter of the Canaanite (or Greek, Syrophenician in Mark) woman. He claims that he has come only to help the "lost sheep of the house of Israel." But then he changes his mind! The instant in which he thus changed his mind was the instant in which the mission of Jesus became "catholic"—changed from being directed to a limited kinship group, the house of Israel, to all humanity independent of kinship group.

What was Jesus expressing in his words "I am not sent but unto the lost sheep of Israel?" Israel was a kinship group. Jacob, or Israel, the saga indicated, had two wives and two concubines. By adding the significant component that a man could have children, the saga could then combine into a single kinship group the presumptive offspring of Leah, Rachel, Bilhah, and Zilpah. Indeed, by pushing the kinship through male lineage backward to Abraham and Isaac, the saga had even combined the Moabites, the Ammonites, the Edomites, and the Ishmaelites into a kinship pattern, providing the basis for some kind of unification among the offspring of various other eponymous male ancestors, Lot, Ishmael, and Esau. But Jesus, the descendant of David by male lineage and yet not the biological son of his father Joseph (and to add to the pathos and credibility of his mission, the descendant of Ruth, a Moabitess and not of Israel), extends his mission beyond the house of Israel.

Patrilineality had served an important purpose in the millenium before Jesus: It made possible the unification of a state beyond the limits set by the matrilineal descent. By the eponymous Leah, the kingdom of the south could be unified. By the eponymous Rachel, the kingdom of the north could be unified. By making both of them wives of Israel, the two kingdoms could be joined. And by making the people of the outlying areas the children of the eponymous Zilpah and Bilhah, the handmaidens of Leah and Rachel and concubines of Israel, the unification could extend even further.

Having been witness to the devastating exile of the northern kingdom, in which the political unity of the people disintegrated through encouragement of violations of the established marital patterns, the exiles of the southern kingdom in Babylon reaffirmed the value of patrilineality as a way of maintaining political unity even in the face of exile. Thus the patrilineal marital pattern had value for political unity not only in the land but also in the face of losing the land. However, by the time of Jesus, after centuries of occupation by Greeks and Romans, the value of the tight social ties in the name of kinship through Israel was coming into doubt. Thus Jesus first says that he has come only to the Israelites and then changes his mind.

Another paradox of the history of Christianity through to the modern period is that, while the Christian version of unification of people through faith rather than kinship made possible the unification of disparate groups throughout the civilized world, the value of patrilineality in achieving unity was also maintained and nurtured throughout the Christian world. Both means of unification prevailed. Indeed, one simple way of conceptualizing the premodern development of Western civilization is in terms of the conflict between unification through faith and unification through patrilineal kinship.

The conflict still prevails, not least in contemporary America. Blacks are one kinship group, whites another. The claim for racial equality in America could perhaps not have been better expressed than by the Christian Martin Luther King. The essential basis of his plea for civil rights was that the Christian idea superseded the kinship idea as the basis for the fundamental identity of human beings.

THE FUTURE

I am tempted, in bringing this essay to a close, to engage in prophecy. Prophecy means prediction and prophecy means prescription. Prediction is difficult because we are deep within one of the major transitional periods in the history of the world. What characterizes the world at the present time is more the boundless possibilities that it contains than easily recognizable and identifiable trends. There are numerous tendencies, but there is no way to determine how the tendencies will fuse into historical trends.

If the trends are weak and the tendencies and possibilities are numerous, then our sphere of decision is enlarged. The commitment to social design, which characterized most of the contributors to the Bible, is something we should emulate. It is true that they ascribed the work of social design to God and saw the expression of the design largely in terms of commandment. Today it is time to take back the burden of social design. It is for us to fashion appropriate arrangements among ourselves so that we may live. It is especially incumbent upon us to find ways of overcoming the great outrage of all human history, that some people thrive at the expense of the neglect, oppression, and diminution—sometimes to the point of death—of others. The great technologies that have been developed over the last centuries provide the possibility that never again. for all the millenia to come, need anyone suffer from lack of maintenance, protection, and education; never again will humanity have to trade the neglect, oppression, and diminution of some for the maintenance, protection, education, liberty, and enhancement of others. But to achieve that, a giant step in social design, a giant step in the arrangements among people, will be required.

The biblical authors had joined the existential longings of human beings to their sexual and reproductive functions. They recognized that the existential problems of origins and death of the individual could be solved by fixing the ego of the individual within the larger historical destiny of the succession of biological life cycles. The biblical writers saw the horror of attempting to cope with human existential longings by sex, on the one hand, and the sacrifice of children, on the other. They sought to overcome that trade-off. They sometimes lost their sense of history, reconceptualizing forever as an eternity which was somehow outside of time. Sometimes they conceived of the human group to which they belonged too narrowly, for too often the arrangements of power and property serve some subgroups at the expense of other. Efforts of mixed success to expand the concept to larger and larger groups, however, characterize the Judeo-Christian tradition. It is now time to perceive the true human identity of all people on the planet. It is time for the recognition that existence can be redeemed—that existential longings can be satisfactorily satisfied—only by fixing the individual's ego within the history and future of all human beings.

The development of social organization around the sexual and reproductive unit, as indicated in the Bible, achieved its successes for a good portion of Western history. Some time around the period of the Renaissance and Reformation it began to give way. The renewed doctrine of predestination of Calvin saw grace and damnation assigned on an individual basis, quite independent of any particular kinship tie. The biblically influenced patrilineal pattern became odious because of its relationship to aristocracy. John Locke, whose thought had a powerful influence in the development of democracy in Europe and America, in the first of his *Two Treatises on Civil Government* of 1690 harshly criticized a book by Robert Filmer entitled *Patriarcha*. Filmer, drawing heavily on biblical authority, had defended the divine right of kings and the supporting patriarchal forms of social organization. Locke challenged the divine right of kings, the authority of the husband over his wife, and the authority of parents over children. At least from that time to the present the centrality of the family organization has been declining. And recently several observers have seriously questioned the family's continued existance.[3]

Yet, recognizing all the faults, let us not renounce the family too quickly. It still remains the major locus of intimacy and protection against the brutal, dehumanizing aspects of our larger bureaucratic —and neglecting, oppressing, and diminshing—forms of social organization. It is, indeed, our major refuge. No bureaucratic institutional form has yet emerged that can compete with it in the rearing of children. The failing of the modern world, as I see it, is that, in the fabulous growth of other institutional structures since the Renaissance and the Reformation, there has been insufficient explicit support from those new institutions for the family.

Nor is there much merit in the complete deregulation of sexual behavior. No society has ever existed without the regulation of sexual behavior in some way, for unregulated sexual behavior invariably produces conflicts that contaminate and degrade all other forms of social interaction.

The abiding contingency of the welfare of the total society on the quality of individual human beings, and the contingency of the quality of human beings on appropriate care, especially in childhood, will be with us throughout all future millenia. What is emerging—and I risk this prediction—is a collective society more dependent on the quality of individual human beings that compose it than ever before in the history of civilization. What was long known, and what was given renewed affirmation by modern psychology, is that the quality of people is the product of appropriate attention to their persons in childhood and adulthood. The text to which I have given my attention in this essay constituted an important step in improving human quality by making men into carers for children and facilitating large-scale social organization. Hopefully, one might look back millenia from now to a record of continued progress in the quality of the human occupants of this planet.

The responses that human beings make even out of noble motives do not necessarily remain noble indefinitely. I have made the argument that the social patterns of the biblical saga were in the direction of bringing about a condition of greater care for children. It does not follow that we should go back to such patterns blindly. The worship of any social institution can be as idolatrous as the worship of gods made by men. The author of the apocryphal Wisdom of Solomon deeply understood how even the great love that a father may have for his child can be the origin of evil:

For the idea of making idols was
    the beginning of fornication,
and the invention of them was the
    corruption of life,
for neither have they existed from
    the beginning
nor will they exist for ever.
For through the vanity of men
    they entered the world,
and therefore their speedy end has
    been planned.
For a father, consumed with grief
    at an untimely bereavement,
made an image of his child, who
    had been suddenly taken from
    him;
and he now honored as a god
    what was once a dead human
    being,
and handed on to his dependents
    secret rites and initiations.
Then the ungodly custom, grown
    strong with time, was kept as a
    law,
and at the command of monarchs
    graven images were worshipped.
When men could not honor
    monarchs in their presence,
    since they lived at a distance,
they imagined their appearance
    far away,
and made a visible image of the
    king whom they honored,
so that by their zeal they might
    flatter the absent one as though
    present.
Then the ambition of the craftsman
    impelled
even those who did not know the

king to intensify their worship.
For he, perhaps wishing to please
  his ruler,
skillfully forced the likeness to take
  more beautiful form,
and the multitude, attracted by the
  charm of his work,
now regarded as an object of
  worship the one whom shortly
  before they had honored as a
  man.
And this became a hidden trap for
  mankind,
because men, in bondage to
  misfortune or to royal authority,
bestowed on objects of stone or
  wood the name that ought not
  to be shared.
Afterward it was not enough for
  them to err about the knowledge
  of God,
but they live in great strife due to
  ignorance,
and they call such great evils
  peace.
For whether they kill children in
  their initiations, or celebrate
  secret mysteries,
or hold frenzied revels with strange
  customs,
they no longer keep either their
  lives or their marriages pure,
but they either treacherously kill
  one another, or grieve one
  another by adultery,
and all is a raging riot of blood and
  murder, theft and deceit,
  corruption, faithlessness, tumult,
  perjury,

> confusion over what is good,
>   forgetfulness of favors,
> pollution of souls, sex perversion,
> disorder in marriage, adultery, and
>   debauchery.
> (The Wisdom of Solomon 14:12–26, RSV)

Idolatry is indeed the great danger, and the major sin. Idolatry is the worship of human creations. In the passage above the author has outlined the development of idolatry. It begins, true enough, with the love of a father for his child. That father, who was invested with commitment to his child, is "consumed with grief at an untimely bereavement." So he fashions an image of that dead child with his own hands, and he honors "as a god what was once a dead human being." And he develops around that a variety of "secret rites and initiations." The "ungodly custom" grows and is "kept as law." The pattern of worshipping what is not present but is only represented by an image is seized upon by monarchs. The worship of absent children becomes the pattern for the worship of absent rulers. The craftsmen enter. They add an aesthetic dimension to the image. They flatter their rulers and suggest a divine quality for them. The populace is thereby entrapped because they "bestowed on objects of stone or wood the name that ought not to be shared."

And in this dynamic what started out as a noble grief of a man for his dead child becomes converted into a pattern in which men "kill children in their initiations." Grief for a dead child ironically turns into an ideology that encourages the killing of more children. The love of life associated with the love of a father for his child is transformed into a love of death.

Notes

1. R. Landes and M. Zborowski, "Hypotheses Concerning the Eastern Jewish Family," *Psychiatry* 13 (1950): 447–464.
2. I have previously argued that the *Book of Job* is the major transitionary docu-

ment to the New Testament. See D. Bakan, *Disease, Pain and Sacrifice* (Boston: Beacon Press, 1971).

3. See David Cooper, *The Death of the Family* (New York: Vintage, 1971); Germaine Greer, *The Female Eunuch* (New York: McGraw-Hill, 1971); Barrington Moore, Jr., *Political Power and Social Theory* (Cambridge, Mass.: Harvard University Press, 1958); Warren Bennis and Philip Slater, *The Temporary Society* (New York: Harper & Row, 1968).

Index